TRUTH THAT TRANSFORMS: A STUDY IN CHRISTIAN DOCTRINE

LAY ACTION MINISTRY PROGRAM
5827 S. Rapp St.
Littleton, CO 80120

David C. Cook Publishing Co.
850 N. Grove Ave.
Elgin, IL 60120

Scripture quotations, unless otherwise noted, are taken from the *Holy Bible: New International Version*, Copyright 1978, 1984 by the International Bible Society, used by permission of Zondervan Bible Publishers.

David C. Cook Publishing Co.
850 North Grove Avenue
Elgin, IL 60120
Printed in U.S.A.

Editor: Gary Wilde
Designer: Chris Patchel
Cover: Lois Rosio Sprague

ISBN: 0-89191-486-2
Library of Congress Catalog Number: 89-81112

TABLE OF CONTENTS

PREFACE

In order to get the "big picture" about Bible doctrine, and understand the relationship of one doctrine to another, picture a tree. We will start our study by examining theological roots, then trunk, and finally branches.

The tree's *root* system is foundational. Thus our study begins by examining the existence and nature of **God**. Next comes the *trunk* of the tree—which we liken to the **Scriptures**. The *branches* then represent the various **truths** taught in Scripture.

And may we add some more? The leaves and fruit speak of what God is doing even today—through the lives of Christians. That's what makes this study exciting and relevant. The Creator of all truth wants to work through us! That's the greatest honor we could ever have. And an awesome responsibility.

First of all, what do we mean by doctrine? *The Concise Dictionary of Christian Theology*, by Millard Erickson, defines doctrine as "a belief or teaching regarding theological themes . . . ." As we proceed through this course we will be looking at who God is, what He has done, and what He teaches us through His Word, the Bible.

Secondly, why should anyone take a course on doctrines? Isn't reading the Bible enough? What benefit will there be for your life? Such a study is beneficial because:

•Christianity is founded not only on personal experience but also on a message—the story of Jesus Christ. Doctrines explain this story and its message in a clear and understandable way;

•Doctrines hold the Christian community together by giving us common ground concerning our faith, belief, and worship;

•Through a study of doctrines we have a basis for the way we are to live our lives. Scripture is our guide to proper relationships with God, other believers, and the world. Through these truths we can determine how God desires us to live out our lives.

Finally, does every Christian agree on all doctrines? Frankly, the history and division of the Christian Church shows that not all Christians interpret passages of Scripture the same. Well-meaning, knowledgeable, and godly persons have debated the meaning of many Scripture passages. Throughout the course of these lessons we shall call upon these various perspectives and compare them to the Biblical data, so that we may decide for ourselves how to interpret the Scripture.

One last note before proceeding on our journey of studying Biblical doctrines. In order to maintain the integrity of the truths of Scripture, we have frequently included extended passages of Scripture for you to read. This was deemed necessary for two primary reasons:

First, in order to grasp the full meaning of a passage, we often need to look at the context in which it is written. Large sections of Scripture are devoted to a number of doctrines, and a careful look at the overall teaching will enhance our understanding of those doctrines. Every verse in the passage may not directly relate to the doctrine, but seeing the "big picture" is important.

Second, other doctrines are only found in short segments of Scripture. And while no less important than those in extended passages, these doctrines need to be supported by looking at a greater number of passages. We include most of the significant texts for each doctrine, while often adding a number of other passages that don't require your specific responses. While it isn't essential for you to look up every supplemental passage listed, we provide them as a resource for the time they may come in handy.

These additional verses guard against a common misuse of the Bible known as "proof-texting," or building a doctrine or belief from Scripture based on a single verse that is typically pulled out of context. You are encouraged in your study of God's Word to examine not only these verses offered but other texts relevant to the same doctrine so that you may be "rooted and grounded in Him, strengthened in the faith you were taught, and overflowing with thankfulness" (Colossians 2:7).

LAY ACTION
MINISTRY PROGRAM

LAMP courses are based on the HEAD, HEART, and HANDS approach to learning. HEAD represents Bible content that you want to know. HEART represents your personal application of the truth. HANDS refers to the LAMP goal of preparing you to use course content in the lives of other people—imparting to others what you have learned (see II Tim. 2:2).

Truth that Transforms can be a powerful instrument of God in your life. If you diligently study each lesson, this course can give you a grip on Bible doctrine that will establish and strengthen your own life, as well as give you a ministry tool to serve God more effectively.

How to Use This Material

This course is for every Christian who is willing to put forth the effort in personal study. But we want you to know "up front" what it is going to cost you in terms of time and commitment. It is going to cost you a good hour of home study for each lesson. Make every effort to spend this much time as a minimum requirement. Also, in order to maximize your personal study time during the week, faithful attendance at the group meetings should be considered a top priority. Not only will you benefit from this group interaction, but the others attending will gain as well.

How to Use This Course

Prepare one lesson each week, in preparation for a weekly group meeting. The weekly group meeting features a *discussion* of the lesson you have studied during the week. It also includes other elements to encourage group life and to guide group members toward personal application of the material.

The group meeting should be *at least* a full hour in length. It should be led by a person who enjoys leading discussions and helping people learn. The leader will study the lesson in the same way as anyone else in the group. In addition, a Leader's Guide provides specific suggestions for conducting each weekly group meeting. This Leader's Guide can be obtained from the address provided on the title page.

Acknowledgments

Many people have been involved in the writing of this course, which has its beginnings in Bible doctrine classes I taught to students in the Philippine Missionary Institute. I am grateful to all of my teachers of theology over the years, but especially to the demands of the inductive approach to the study of Scripture. Such studies have assisted in the development of this course. Most recently, I have appreciated the help that Kelly Moore, now serving in Kenya, has given in helping shape some of this material.

1

THE EXISTENCE AND NATURE OF GOD

A Russian cosmonaut once traveled for some time around the earth in a tiny space capsule. After completing his mission, he is said to have triumphantly declared: "I have searched the heavens and didn't find God anywhere." Clearly, in his mind, God did not exist. On the other hand, Gemini astronaut James A. McDivitt, after circling the earth 62 times, reported: "I did not see God looking into my space-cabin window...but I could recognize His work in the stars."

No one has ever seen an atom. Yet the belief that the universe is entirely made up of atoms is universally accepted. Why? Because all of the scientific evidence points to the fact that atoms must exist. In the same way, no one has ever seen God. Yet there is much evidence to be found for His existence.

The Existence of God

How do we know that God exists? The Bible nowhere sets forth a statement proving His existence. Rather it everywhere *assumes* that He does exist. From the perspective of the Bible writers, God *needs* no proof. How is this statement verified in Genesis 1:1?

The Bible does, however, speak of one key evidence for

God's existence. Read Psalm 19:1-4. The evidence all humankind has that there is a God is:

_____

Paul brings out this same truth in Romans 1:18-20. What is it that can be known about God from creation?

_____

_____

What did humankind do with this knowledge? (see vss. 21-23)

_____

_____

What do men and women often do today with this knowledge of God? Why?

_____

_____

What parts of God's creative work especially impress you?

_____

How can this be used as an opportunity for witness?

_____

_____

For those whose hearts and minds are open, the created world—from the mind-boggling expanse of the universe, to the amazing intricacies of a single cell—proclaims the existence of its Creator and provides irrefutable evidence of His existence.

Ponder the words of Galileo, the most profound philosopher of his age who, when questioned by the Roman Inquisition as to his belief in the existence of God, pointed to a straw on the dungeon floor and replied that from the structure of that object alone he could infer with certainty the existence of an intelligent Creator. Would that we also would see our Creator in *all* His handiwork!

The Nature of God

Many years ago a missionary was seeking to explain what God is like. He told a story about three blind men who had just encountered an elephant for the first time and were sharing what they had learned about this amazing creature. The first man, touching the elephant's side, described it as being like a hairy wall. The second had felt its trunk, and likened it to a tree. The third had grabbed hold of its tail, and described it as a rope. Each one had felt a part of the animal, and each was right—at least partly so.

What is God like? Since the Bible tells us many things about what God is like, and since it is vital that we know them, we will devote our first two lessons to the study of the nature and character of God.

GOD IS PERFECT. Everything said about God presupposes and amplifies the fact that God is absolute and perfect. How is His perfection brought out in each of the following passages?

Deuteronomy 32:4 _____

Psalm 19:7 _____

Psalm 18:30 _____

Ecclesiastes 3:14 _____

Matthew 5:48 _____

I once heard a young man say, "If God were perfect, I'd worship him." How might we help him see this truth?

_____

_____

GOD IS ONE. The Bible contains many references to the fact

13

that there is only one God. One of the most well-known is Deuteronomy 6:4, which says:

_____

This means that God is one in His essential being. This doctrine does not, however, exclude the possibility of the *Trinity* of God, a subject we will examine in the next lesson. Some additional references to the oneness of God are: Isaiah 43:10, 11; 44:6; I Corinthians 8:4; Ephesians 4:6; and I Timothy 2:5.

Bible-believing Christians, then, hold to a *monotheistic* view of God. The Biblical doctrine of the oneness of God stands distinct from *polytheism*, which teaches that there are many gods; from *tritheism*, which teaches that there are three Gods (Father, Son, and Holy Spirit), and from a strict *dualism*, which teaches that there are two equal and rudimentary forces in the world, those of good and of evil.

GOD IS SPIRIT. The Bible does not attempt to define God. The closest it comes to this is in Jesus' encounter with the Samaritan woman in John 4. What important application of this truth (that God is spirit) does Jesus make in verse 24?

_____

Yet the Bible does talk about God's "arm," "ear," and "face" in Isaiah 59:1, 2 and other passages. In light of John 4:24, what meaning would you give to these references to a physical body?

_____

_____

The Bible also refers to God as spirit in II Corinthians 3. What effect is the Lord who "is the Spirit" to have in *our* lives as Christians? (vss. 17, 18)

_____

_____

14

Here in II Corinthians 3 Paul strongly contrasts the Old Covenant with the New. The Spirit's life-transforming power through Christ has rendered the Old Testament Law obsolete in terms of its supposed ability to make us righteous before God.

GOD IS A PERSONALITY. That is, God demonstrates many characteristics also found in humans. How do we know this? (Gen. 1:26) Because:

_____

Since we have already learned that God is spirit, this "image" must refer to something other than God's physical form. It must therefore refer to His personality.

Three basic aspects of personality are: *intellect*, *emotions*, and *will*. Three elements of God's intelligence include: knowledge (I Sam. 2:3); understanding (Job 28:20-23); and wisdom (Prov. 3:19, 20; Isaiah 11:2). A variety of God's emotions can be found throughout Scripture: love (Jer. 31:3); hate (Ps. 5:5); anger (Rom. 1:18); sorrow (Isa. 53:3); compassion (Lam. 3:22); and many others. Finally, we see in God's will a plan and purpose for the created universe and mankind. Because of His steadfastness and faithfulness, what He has set out to do will come about (see Isa. 46: 9-10; Mt. 6:10). Which of God's personality traits do you find in the following sample verses:

Romans 12:1 _____

Psalm 111:4 _____

Proverbs 3:19 _____

Besides the three verses studied above, choose one verse from the preceding paragraph that tells of God's personality and describe how you can personally relate to God because of it.

_____

_____

GOD IS A *LIVING* PERSONALITY. The Old Testament frequently emphasizes this truth. Why? Look for a practical reason in Joshua 3:10 and I Samuel 17:26.

_____

_____

How does this truth help you today?

_____

_____

GOD'S NAMES HELP DESCRIBE HIS PERSONALITY. A Christian worker named Rev. Achenhead once spoke in our church. We thought his name amusing but he passed it off, saying, "What's in a name, anyway?" But Biblically speaking, names are very important. The names of God help us understand more about what God is like. The Hebrew names for God are listed in three categories: general names, covenant name, and particular names.

A. General Names

El (singular) has "strength" as its underlying thought, and occurs some 250 times in the Old Testament. Most frequently it occurs in connection with other words, such as *El Elyon*, "the Most High God," the object of our reverence and worship (Gen. 14:18-22); and *El Shaddai*, "God Almighty," suggesting God's greatness as a source of comfort and blessing for His people (Gen. 17:1).

Elohim (plural) occurs over 2,000 times, and implies "the God of creation," "Providence," and "the Supreme Ruler." The use of this word for God indicates that He is strong and mighty and should therefore be feared. *Elohim* is used for God in Genesis 1:1.

B. The Covenant Name

Jehovah (or *Yahweh*, as many scholars believe it was pronounced) is God's special name with Israel, and occurs some 7,000 times in the Old Testament. It means "the Self-Existent One." Its origin and meaning is indicated in

Exodus 3:14, 15, expressing the fact that He is always the same, especially unchangeable in His covenant relationship. Jehovah will always fulfill His promises.

C. Particular Names

Some names occur in combination with *Jehovah* (or *Yahweh*), such as *Jehovah-Jireh* ("the Lord will provide," Gen. 22:14); *Jehovah-Nissi* ("the Lord, my banner," Exod. 17:15, 16) and *Jehovah-Tsidkenu* ("the Lord our righteousness," Jer. 23:6; 33:16). And finally, the name *Adon* (singular) is used 30 times; and *Adonai* (plural), 280 times. *Adonai* is usually rendered "Lord," the possessor and ruler of all humankind. The New Testament counterpart for *Adonai* is *kurios* (Rev. 4:8).

Look up two or three passages where these names for God occur and share how that particular name encourages you.

_____

_____

_____

_____

Thinking of the people you know, what kinds of questions would they likely ask about God?

_____

_____

_____

_____

_____

2

THE TRINITY
AND ATTRIBUTES OF GOD

Chuck Colson, former White House assistant during Richard Nixon's presidency, wrote a best-selling book titled *Loving God*. Before delving into the subject of our response to God, listen to Mr. Colson's description of western culture:

> *For a generation, Western society has been obsessed with the search for self. We have turned the age-old philosophical question about the meaning and purpose of life into a modern growth industry. Like Heinz, there are fifty-seven varieties: EST, awareness workshops, TA—each fad with an avid following until something new comes along.*
>
> *Popular literature rides the wave with best-selling titles that guarantee success with everything from making money to firming flabby thighs. This not-so-magnificent obsession to "find ourselves" has spawned a whole set of counterfeit values. We worship fame, success, materialism, and celebrity. We want to "live for success" as we "look out for number one," and we don't mind "winning through intimidation."*

Colson goes on to say that the same mindset has infiltrated the church and perverted its message. The insidious disease commonly called "me-ism" has created a "what's-in-it-for-me" gospel. Man—not God—is often the focal point of concentration.

Charles Swindoll emphasizes that pursuing God, not

self-fulfillment, is the route to joy. In *Growing Deep In The Christian Life*, he echoes Colson's concern, and tells how to escape the cultural trap of "me-isms":

I am more convinced than ever that life's major pursuit is not knowing self . . . but knowing God. . . . Unless God is the major pursuit of our lives, all other pursuits are dead-end streets, including trying to know ourselves. They won't work. They won't satisfy. They won't result in fulfillment. They won't do for us what we think they're going to do. You never really begin the process of coming to know yourself until you begin the process of coming to know God.

That's why this doctrine course begins with a focus on God. In Lesson 1, you were introduced to the existence and nature of God. Lesson 2 puts the spotlight on God's triune existence and examines specific attributes that describe Him. Investigating the Bible's portrait of God is crucial. What we believe (or refuse to believe) inevitably translates itself into our actions and attitudes. As A. W. Tozer put it, "What we believe about God is the most important thing about us."

The Trinity of God

The word Trinity can be expressed as tri-unity. It says that the *one* true God consists of Father, Son, and Holy Spirit—one God in three persons.

The trinitarian conception of God is a major point of Christian doctrine, yet the word is not found in the Bible. Shocking? "If this is true," you may ask, "then why is the doctrine so strongly held by virtually the entire Christian Church?" This is a fair question—one that we will look at now, under two categories: implied arguments, and direct arguments.

IMPLIED ARGUMENTS FOR THE TRINITY. The first implied argument comes from the common Hebrew name for God, *Elohim*. Interestingly, this is a uni-plural noun. That is, the word is plural in form, yet is used with a singular meaning when referring to God. Of course, this fact of Hebrew grammar does not prove that God is a Trinity, but it does make it possible.

The word *Elohim* makes possible the doctrine of the Trinity because it is _____.

The second implied argument is that plural pronouns are used in the Creation account. Which pronouns are used in Genesis 1:26? _____ Yet contrast verse 27, where God said that He created man in_____
_____. (Compare also Gen. 11:7 and Isa. 6:8.)

How do you understand this plural/singular use of pronouns for God?

_____

While these implied arguments are not conclusive, they show that the Biblical writers referred to God as more than a simple unity and point to the possibility of a Trinity.

DIRECT ARGUMENTS FOR THE TRINITY. While the Bible does not directly state that God is a Trinity, it *does* teach that the Father, the Son, and the Spirit are all equally God.

Clearly, the Father is God. The Bible is replete with references to God the Father. See Jeremiah 31:9; John 6:27; Galatians 1:1, 3; Ephesians 4:6; Hebrews 12:9; and James 1:17.

Summarize the truths taught in these Scriptures:

_____

Similarly, Scripture teaches that Jesus is God. In John 8:52-58 Jesus confronted the unbelieving Jews and made an amazing statement about who He was. As you read this passage, focus on verse 58. Not only did Jesus claim to have existed before _____ (who lived some 2,000 years earlier), but He also claimed_____

_____.

Now turn to Exodus 3:14 and express your understanding of what Jesus meant by this statement in verse 58.

_____

Next, turn back to John 14:8-11. Notice how Jesus responded to Philip's question "Lord, show us the Father." What was Jesus teaching about who He was?

_____

In John 10:30 Jesus said: _____.
It is interesting to note that the structure of the Greek in this passage indicates a oneness in *being*—not just in *purpose*. The Jews would not have objected to Jesus' claim to be "one in purpose" with God, for they also made this claim. What *did* they understand Jesus to mean (vs. 33)?

_____

The above passages clearly teach that:

_____

Scripture also teaches that the Holy Spirit is God. From the following passages note the aspect of God's *nature* which the Spirit also possesses.

Psalm 139:7-11 _____

Hebrews 9:14 _____

I Corinthians 2:10, 11 _____

With what *work* of God is the Spirit identified in the following verses?

Psalm 104:30 _____

II Peter 1:21 _____

John 3:5 _____

To conclude, turn to Deuteronomy 6:4 and describe the Trinity of God in *your* understanding.

_____

Since there is only one God, the conclusion reached by the early church councils was that God must be a unity in three persons—thus the term Trinity developed.

ILLUSTRATIONS OF THE TRINITY. Many illustrations have been used to help explain the Trinity. Here are a few that have been helpful to others:

Time is past, present, and future. There can be no past without the present, nor any future without the present. This is unity. However, the past is not the present, nor is the present the future. This is trinity.

Space has width, length, and height. Each is a part of the other, thus there is unity. But each is distinct from the other, thus a trinity.

Water can be a liquid, a vapor, or a solid. While water is not strictly a vapor, nor ice, yet all three are H_2O.

While these examples may give us a *better* understanding of God's three-in-oneness, we realize that with our finite minds we must sometimes accept what we don't fully understand.

TRUTH YOU CAN USE. If you should be talking with someone who does not believe in the Trinity, yet is willing to accept the evidence of Scripture, first point to the existence of three persons in the Deity. Don't attempt to explain the Trinity until the person has first accepted the deity of Christ and the deity of the Holy Spirit.

Reflecting back on what you have just learned about the Trinity, select one key passage showing that:

• the Father is God _____

• the Son is God _____

• the Spirit is God _____

The Attributes of God

What is meant by the term "attribute"? Webster defines it as "an inherent characteristic." Thus, God's attributes are those characteristics that are part of God's nature. Let's zero in on some of the attributes of God.

GOD IS ETERNAL. How is this truth expressed by the Psalmist in Psalm 103:25-27?

_____

GOD IS OMNIPRESENT. This means that God is present everywhere, at all times. How is this truth expressed in the following passage?

Jeremiah 23:23, 24 _____

How can this truth about God help in your life? Look at Psalm 139:7-12 as you work through your response.

_____

_____

GOD IS OMNISCIENT. God knows everything—not only all facts, but how to use all the facts. God's omniscience is seen in Psalm 139:1-4. What is the down-to-earth value of God's omniscience in:

Proverbs 15:3 _____

Hebrews 4:13 _____

Romans 8:28 _____

How does God's omniscience help _you_ in making right choices?

_____

GOD IS OMNIPOTENT. This means that God is all-powerful. The Hebrew _El Shaddai_ means "all-powerful" or "all-sufficient." This name was first used by God as He spoke to Abraham in Genesis 17:1. Let's turn the spotlight on Abraham for a few minutes.

Many years earlier God had promised him that: "a son coming from your own body will be your heir" (Gen. 15:4). Yet the years kept rolling by and Abraham, now nearing

100 years old, still had no son. In the midst of this stressful time God revealed Himself as *El Shaddai*, "God Almighty." To Sarah, now long past child-bearing age, the Lord asked: "Is anything too hard for the Lord?" (Gen. 18:14).

It's a question worth pondering isn't it? In the space below, write down one "impossible" concern you have, followed by your prayer to the "God of the impossible."

_____

_____

_____

_____

On what *basis* does Jeremiah confidently pray, "Nothing is too hard for you"? (Jer. 32:17)

_____

GOD IS HOLY. The basic meaning of the Greek word for "holy" is "separation." God is completely separate from anything that is not pure. The Bible's teaching about the holiness of God is emphatic and consistent throughout Scripture. For example, see Exodus 15:11; I Samuel 2:2; Isaiah 57:15; Hebrews 7:26. Isaiah uses the term "the Holy One" some 30 times.

How does the holiness of God influence our lives as Christians (I Pet. 1:15, 16)?

_____

God's holiness means He is _____

_____.

GOD IS RIGHTEOUS. The righteousness of God is also a common theme of Scripture. Righteousness can be defined as the perfect agreement between the nature of God and His acts. How is God's righteousness demonstrated in Psalm 119:137; 129:4 and 145:17?

_____

Read Jeremiah 12:1. What was Jeremiah's problem?

_____

How does God's righteousness influence us as believers, according to I John 2:29 and 3:7?

_____

Because God is righteous (just), we know He will a) keep His promises; b) judge those who do wrong; c) forgive us as we repent of our wrongdoing. What an encouragement!

GOD IS LOVE. The apostle John states this truth very simply when he says, "God is love" (I Jn. 4:8, 16). How did God's love for the world express itself? (See John 3:16 and Romans 5:8.)

_____

How is our behavior to be affected by Christ's love for us in I John 3:16-18?

_____

_____

Some attributes are really expressions of God's love. These include: mercy, grace, longsuffering, and goodness. Let's look briefly at each of these.

God is *Merciful*. The mercy (or compassion) of God is mentioned in such verses as Exodus 34:6; Deuteronomy 4:31; II Corinthians 1:3 and Ephesians 2:4. Because of God's mercy He holds back from us what we deserve and provides us with that which we don't deserve.

According to Isaiah 55:7, how may the wicked receive God's mercy?

_____

How has God shown mercy to you recently?

_____

God is *Gracious*. Peter speaks of "the God of all grace"

25

(I Pet. 5:10). And in Ephesians 3:2 Paul reminds the Ephesians of "the administration of God's grace"—that is, that the Gentiles should also be recipients of God's grace. To whom does God give His grace (Prov. 3:34)?

_____

With what result (Eph. 2:8, 9)?

_____

God is *Longsuffering*, or patient. This means that God delays the punishment that ought to be received by sinful men. Why is God patient with such men (II Pet. 3:9)?

_____

God is *Good*. "The Lord is good, a refuge in times of trouble. He cares for those who trust in him" (Nahum 1:7).

How can we enjoy God's goodness (Ps. 34:8)?

_____

What does this mean?

_____

_____

God's love is also expressed in His:

_____   _____

_____   _____

What This Means to Me

The practical implications of each divine attribute were considered as you proceeded through this Bible study. Right now, take one additional step in the direction of application. Review the list of God's attributes and jot down any insights you have about how they might increase your desire to worship:

The Trinity of God _____

_____

26

The omnipresence of God _____

_____

The omniscience of God _____

_____

The omnipotence of God _____

_____

The holiness of God _____

_____

The righteousness of God _____

_____

The love of God _____

_____

1. Which attribute of God encourages you most? Why?

_____

_____

_____

2. Which attribute of God is most *convicting*? Why?

_____

_____

_____

3. Which attribute, if fully comprehended, would make the most significant impact on your daily experience? Explain your answer.

_____

_____

_____

3

THE AUTHORITY AND INSPIRATION OF SCRIPTURE

Years ago, evangelist Billy Graham described a turning point in his public ministry:

In 1949 I had been having a great many doubts concerning the Bible. I was . . . [finding] apparent contradictions in Scripture. Some things I could not reconcile with my restricted concept of God. When I stood up to preach, the authoritative *note so characteristic of all great preachers of the past was lacking.*

Like hundreds of other young students of the Bible, I was waging the intellectual battle of my life. The outcome could certainly affect my future ministry. I remember almost wrestling with God. I dueled with my doubts, and my soul seemed to be caught in the crossfire.

Finally, in desperation, I surrendered my will to the living God revealed in Scripture. I knelt before my open Bible and said, "Lord, many things in this book I don't understand. But you have said, "The just shall live by faith. Here and now, by faith, I accept the Bible as Your Word. I take it without reservations. Where there are things I cannot understand, I will reserve judgment until I receive more light. If this pleases You, give me authority as I proclaim Your Word, and through that authority convict them of sin and turn sinners to Christ."

Within six weeks we started our Los Angeles Crusade, which is now history. During that Crusade I discovered the secret that changed my ministry. I stopped trying to prove that the Bible was true. I had settled in my own mind that it was, and this faith was conveyed to the audience. Over and over I found myself saying, "The Bible says . . ." I felt as though I were merely a voice through which the Holy Spirit was speaking.

It was as if I had a rapier in my hands, and through the power of the Bible, was slashing deeply into men's consciences, leading them to surrender to God.

—from "A Rapier In My Hand," *Radiant Tidings* magazine, Summer 1973.

Billy Graham discovered that our attitude toward God's Word affects our life and ministry. Without confidence in Scripture, motivation for holiness and service wanes. That's why this course devotes an entire lesson to the authority and inspiration of Scripture. Though an act of faith is required, as illustrated by Billy Graham's experience, we have valid reasons for trusting the Bible. When we accept God's Word as true, we aren't committing intellectual suicide. Though evidence for the Bible's reliability exists elsewhere, Lesson 3 focuses on what Jesus and the Apostles said about its trustworthiness.

This lesson deals with two vital topics: the *inspiration* of Scripture and the *authority* of Scripture. (Note: Key ideas in this lesson are based on E.M.B. Green's *The Authority of Scripture* [Falcon Booklets, London].)

The Authority of Scripture

Many years ago, Richard Hooker, one of the great English theologians, noted three possible sources of authority for Christian life and doctrine. These are: the Christian Bible, the Christian Church (tradition), and Christian reason.

Some branches of the Church today tend to emphasize one or another of these three authorities. Some emphasize the place of *Tradition*, looking back to the writings of the early church fathers, the councils, the creeds, episcopal pronouncements, and the development of worship practices through the centuries as evidence of God's working among His people. In this view, the Church itself is the final basis of authority.

But the Reformers of the 16th century saw what could happen when church leadership let the importance of Tradition overshadow the influence of the Bible. They saw man-made formulas and legalisms creeping in that went contrary to Scriptural teaching. Thus, the Reformers pushed for a return to the *Bible* as the ultimate authority, and evangelical churches today hold to this emphasis.

In more recent years certain theologians have downgraded the authority of both the Church and the Bible and instead give authority to judge truth to their own *human reason*.

These three possible bases for the Christian's authority are talked about in the New Testament. In Jesus' day, two prominent religious groups were the Pharisees and the Sadducees. They believed quite different things about the authority for their faith.

THE AUTHORITY OF TRADITION. The Pharisees were the dominant religious party in Jesus' day. They practiced literally hundreds of rules daily which were not in their Scriptures. They were *added* to those commands given by Moses. These traditions came to have powerful authority over every detail of their lives. The purpose of these rules was good—to protect people from transgressing God's Law. Notice, however, how these traditions were frequently *practiced* in Jesus' day. To do this turn to Mark 7.

What was the problem that had developed? (vss. 1-5)

_____

_____

What was actually wrong with these traditions? (vs. 7)

_____

For the Jews, what was the effect of the traditions on the actual Commandments of God which they were supposed to protect? (vss. 8-13)

_____

What in this passage shows that this was not an isolated case?

_____

What do you believe Jesus would teach about the place of traditions in the Church today?

_____

_____

John R. Stott, while not denying that we should maintain some traditions in our churches today (and every church has some) stated:

Ultimate authority is in Scripture, in God speaking through Scripture, whereas tradition is oral, open and often self-contradictory.

What do you feel about the place and importance of Tradition in the church?

_____

_____

What are some traditions that you feel have either helped or hindered Christian life in churches you've attended?

_____

_____

_____

THE AUTHORITY OF REASON. The Sadducees were another powerful religious body in Jesus' day. They differed significantly from the Pharisees, in that they accepted only the authority of the Law, contained in the first five books

31

of the Bible. Jesus' encounter with these religious leaders is highly instructive as well. To join this encounter, read Matthew 22:23-33.

What illustration did these Sadducees, who did not believe in resurrection, use in arguing against it? (vss. 23-28)

_____

_____

How did Jesus then prove the truth of the resurrection? (vss. 29-32)

_____

_____

The danger of placing the authority of reason above that of Holy Scripture is that we may begin to rationalize away the truths of the Bible—truths we should both believe and follow.

How do you think Jesus would respond today to those who would place human reason above the authority of Scripture?

_____

_____

The Inspiration of Scripture

Once we have established that neither Tradition alone nor reason alone is an adequate basis for our faith, we are ready to look at what Jesus Himself taught about the inspiration (and hence authority) of Scripture.

JESUS' TEACHING ABOUT INSPIRATION. Who did Jesus declare was the author of Scripture?

Matthew 22:31 _____

Mark 7:9-13 _____

Jesus also recognized the entire Old Testament (the only

Scriptures at that time) as from God. In Luke 24:44, He referred to each of its three divisions—the Law of Moses, the Prophets, and the Psalms (the first book of the Writings)—as being a witness to the deeds of Christ which must be fulfilled.

Summarize Jesus' teaching concerning the inspiration of Scripture.

_____

_____

_____

CONTRARY ARGUMENTS. Some scholars have tried to invalidate Jesus' belief in the full inspiration and authority of Scripture by advancing either of the following two theories.

The *Kenosis Theory* teaches that by becoming a human being, Jesus shared in the errors of thinking of the people of His time. Since it was then commonly believed that Scripture was God's Word, Jesus also shared this error— or so goes the theory. Proof for this view, it is said, is found in Philippians 2:5-8. Those advancing this view hold to the claim that Jesus emptied Himself of His essential Godhood while on earth, thereby having the capability to err. However, Dr. Charles Ryrie says that Christ's "emptying" should be understood as, *"The voluntary non-use of certain attributes during His [Jesus'] earthly life."*

Another theory used to try to invalidate Jesus' teaching about the inspiration of the Bible is called the *Accommodation Theory*. This theory teaches that Jesus merely agreed to the erroneous beliefs of the people, accepting their ignorance as a fact of life. If these people believed in an inspired Bible, then He would go along with their belief, even though He knew better—or so the *Accommodation Theory* teaches. We can agree, however, that this viewpoint is totally out of character with Jesus' high ethical and moral teachings.

"You will know the truth, and the truth will set you free" (Jn. 8:32). Jesus confronted error rather than accommodating to it.

THE APOSTLES' TEACHING ABOUT INSPIRATION. All authority in heaven and on earth had been given to Jesus (Mt. 28:18). To preserve and carry out His teaching, Jesus delegated this authority to His apostles, commissioning them to act in His stead. While Jesus Christ gave them the right, the Holy Spirit gave them the power and ability to minister in teaching, preaching, and *writing*. How did Peter compare the writings of the apostles with those of the Old Testament in II Peter 3:2, 16?

_____

_____

According to II Timothy 3:16, 17, how much of Scripture is inspired?

_____

On a practical level, how is this helpful to us?

_____

THE WAY GOD INSPIRED SCRIPTURE. The way God inspired Scripture has been variously defined by theologians. One of these (quoted by Henry Thiessen) is by L. Gaussen, Professor of Systematic Theology, Oratoire, Geneva. He says that inspiration is:

That inexplicable power which the divine Spirit put forth of old on the authors of Holy Scripture . . . even in the employment of the words they used, and to preserve them alike from all error and from all omission.

Scripture on this subject is found in II Peter 1:21: "For prophecy never had its origin in the will of man, but men spoke from God as they were carried along by the Holy Spirit."

34

The Greek word translated "carried along" may be used to describe the action of the wind on a boat, filling the sails and carrying it along on the water. In a similar way, the Holy Spirit moved upon and motivated the writers of Holy Scripture. He did so in such a way that the writing style of individual authors was retained. The Biblical writers, then, were far more than instruments of dictation.

THE EXTENT OF INSPIRATION. To what extent is Scripture inspired? Again, let's look at our Lord's view. What He taught ought to settle the question. Jesus taught that inspiration reaches beyond the ideas of Scripture, to their very words. How did He express this truth in Matthew 5:18?

_____

_____

Paul makes this point in a similar way. In I Corinthians 2:13 he says: "This is what we speak, not in _____ taught us by human wisdom but in _____ taught by the Spirit, expressing spiritual truths in spiritual _____." Paul insisted that God's message came in the words of the written text.

Choose a verse that verifies the inspiration of Scripture. Write this verse below and memorize it. Be prepared to quote it during the next meeting.

_____

_____

_____

_____

_____

THE CREEDS AGREE. The great statements about Christian doctrine which came from the Reformation emphasized the authority of Scripture. For example:

The Holy Scripture alone remains the only judge, rule, and standard according to which all dogmas shall be discerned and judged.
—Lutheran Formula of Concord

Holy Scriptures containeth all things necessary to salvation: so that whatsoever is not read therein, nor may be proved thereby, is not to be required of any man, that it should be believed as an article of the faith.
—The Church of England's sixth article of religion

All the books of the Old and New Testament are given by inspiration of God, to be the rule of faith and life.
—Westminster Confession, an official statement of
  Presbyterian belief

Practical Application

To conclude this lesson, let's highlight the practical value of the truth of Scripture's inspiration for our own lives.

1. We should regard Scripture as being the source of spiritual life and light. See Psalm 119:11, 18.

2. We should look for Christ in the Bible. The study of Scripture should first and foremost lead us to the person of Christ, who alone can give us spiritual life. See Luke 24:27; John 5:39, 40 and I Corinthians 10:4.

3. We need to study the Bible. Since the Bible is the Christian's authority, it is the most important book for us to study. To study means more than just to read. We can read without understanding. But God wants us to understand His Word, so that we may know how to live as He wants. See II Timothy 2:15.

4. We should apply Scripture to our lives. We need to look for those spiritual lessons from all of Scripture which relate to our circumstances and needs. Two important questions we must continually ask as we study the Bible are: What did this mean to the original hearers? and: What does this mean to me? Answering these two questions will help us accurately apply the Word of God to our own lives.

5. We need to obey the Bible. What important advice does James 1:22-25 give us in this regard?

_____

_____

Let us make it a lifetime rule: _Any truth we find in Scripture, we will first apply to our own life._

6. We need to use the Bible in ministry to others. In all ministry contexts, conveying Biblical content is crucial to effectiveness. Why? (Before formulating your answer, read the following verses: Acts 20:32; Rom. 1:16; II Tim. 3:15-17 and Heb. 24:12.)

_____

_____

_____

_____

What follows are typical relational and environmental contexts in which many Christians have opportunities to convey truth or perspectives from God's Word. Put a check mark by two or three of these avenues of service which you feel God may be nudging you to travel in the future:

_____ teaching in the church program
_____ leading a home Bible study
_____ discipling a new believer (one-to-one)
_____ witnessing to an unsaved person
_____ giving a personal testimony
_____ notes of encouragement to Christian workers, or hurting people.

_____ instruction of children in the home
_____ OTHER (Write in an opportunity you're aware of.)

_____

_____

_____

_____

4

THE CREATION
AND FALL OF
HUMANKIND

In his Bible doctrine book for teens titled *You Want Me To Know What?* Terry Powell describes the composition of the human body:

About 70% of your body is water. About 3% is nitrogen. In addition, someone has estimated that the human body contains:
  enough sulphur to rid a dog of fleas
  enough lime to whitewash a chicken coop
  enough fat for six bars of soap
  enough iron for a few dozen nails
  enough phosphorus for 20 boxes of matches
  enough magnesium for one dose of Milk of Magnesia
  enough sugar for 10 cups of coffee
  enough potassium to explode a toy cannon
  enough salt for 20 spoonfuls

That chemical breakdown shows how physically complex and detailed God made us. David put it this way: "Thou didst form my inward parts: Thou didst weave me in my mother's womb. I will give thanks to Thee, for I am fearfully and wonderfully made" (Ps. 139:13, 14, NASB).

We are far more than an intricate combination of chemicals, though. Lesson 4 explains why we are unique among God's creations, and probes the implications of our divine origin. We will also trace the origin and impact of sin on human nature. No course on Bible doctrine is complete without asking, "What does Scripture teach about the human being?"

The Creation Account

The Bible account of creation is recorded in Genesis 1.

What two things set humans apart from all other creatures God made? (see verses 25, 26)

This statement certainly does not seem to indicate that humankind "evolved" and is thus merely a higher state of animal. Concerning the doctrine of the creation of humankind in contrast to the theory of evolution, T.C. Hammond in his well-read *In Understanding Be Men* says:

Genesis 1:26, 27 would have us take the view that man's creation had something unique attached to it. If true science denies this . . . then indeed it is in conflict with revelation. No compromise is possible or desirable.

THE IMAGE OF GOD IN HUMANKIND. The great difference between humankind and the rest of creation, as we have seen, is that humans were created in the "image" and "likeness" of God (Gen. 1:26, 27 and 5:1). In what sense has mankind been made in God's image? It cannot be our physical image, since, as we learned earlier, God is _____. It must therefore relate to our immaterial part—our soul, or spirit.

What the image of God consists of is not entirely clear, although two passages in the New Testament give us a partial answer. What is implied in Colossians 3:10?

Which specific aspects of mankind's likeness to God are mentioned in Ephesians 4:23, 24?

This image however, must consist of more than the righteousness and holiness indicated in this passage, associated with the new nature, for the Genesis account indicates that humankind as a whole is created in God's image. See also I Corinthians 11:7 and James 3:9. Consider the view of Louis Berkhof, who says that Reformed theologians in general believe it to "consist in man's spiritual, rational, moral, and immortal being" (*A Summary of Christian Doctrine*, page 63).

As you witness to your non-Christian friends, what value can you see in knowing that all humankind is made in God's image?

_____

_____

There has been debate among Christian theologians about whether the image of God has been lost as a result of sin. However, the Biblical record indicates many of the same prohibitions and abilities (such as the ability to discern God and know what He requires—see especially Romans 1:19-21) are in all people from the beginning, regardless of their spiritual condition. It is because of this inherent condition that Christ came to earth so that *all* people might be saved. It is God's intention that fellowship, obedience, and love characterize mankind's relationship with God.

BODY, SOUL, AND SPIRIT. Theologians have long discussed whether the human being has two parts (body and soul), or three parts (body, soul, and spirit). Many Bible students see the soul and the spirit as two words used to express the same idea. Others see a fine but important distinction between the soul and the spirit. Which view is suggested in I Thessalonians 5:23 and in Hebrews 4:12?

_____

Inasmuch as theologians differ widely on this subject, it

is probably wise to note that Scripture does not clearly define this matter. In some passages "soul" is identified with the whole of the person—such as at creation, when the first human became a "living being" or soul. Yet, the human soul goes beyond mere physical life. See Matthew 10:28 and Mark 8:36 as examples of this. Further, if an aspect of the soul is spirit, then, strictly speaking, it is a person's spirit which is capable of fellowship with God. See Romans 8:16; Ephesians 6:18 and Hebrews 12:23 for examples.

The Fall of Humankind

The origin of sin in the world is clearly recorded in Genesis 3:1-7. Read through these verses once again. Who was the "serpent" who tempted Eve? Compare Revelation 12:9 and 20:2.

_____

_____

Three steps can be traced in the serpent's method of temptation. First, the serpent cast *doubt* on God's Word ("Did God really say . . . ?" Genesis 3:1). Second, Eve *added* to what God had said ("and you must not touch it," Genesis 3:3). And third, the serpent *denied* what God had said ("You will not surely die," Genesis 3:4).

Can we see the same pattern in Satan's attacks on the Word of God today? What are some things you have heard or know about which:

1. Cause people to have doubts about Scripture?

_____

_____

2. Seek to add to Scripture?

_____

_____

3. Deny the truth of God's Word?

_____

_____

In what ways was Eve tempted? (Gen. 3:6)

_____

Now compare I John 2:16. What does this verse suggest about the approach of Satan in tempting humankind?

_____

_____

What provision has God made for our weaknesses in the following verses?

Hebrews 4:15, 16 _____

I Corinthians 10:13 _____

I John 1:9 _____

THE ORIGIN OF SIN. The question is sometimes asked: "How did sin come into the universe in the first place?" This is another question that cannot be definitely answered from Scripture. But since God is not the author of sin, He could not have made a sinful being—Satan. Therefore Satan must have at some point *become* evil. How did this happen? Many Bible scholars identify Isaiah 14 and Ezekiel 28 with the fall of Satan. We do know, from Jude 6 and II Peter 2:4, that some angels did fall. When we study Lesson 11 we will look at these matters more fully.

THE EFFECTS OF THE FALL. What was an immediate effect noticed by Adam and Eve? (Genesis 3:7)

_____

What else did they do which indicated their fear and shame? (vs. 8)

_____

43

Running away from God is characteristic of people who have something to hide. We seek to hide our evil deeds.

What response did Adam and Eve make to God's questions in verses 11 and 13?

_____

What was God's judgment on the serpent (vss. 14, 15)?

_____

What did God promise Eve (vs. 16)?

_____

How did their sin affect Adam's environment (vss. 17-19)?

_____

_____

God's promise of death if they ate the fruit (2:17) has two aspects. First, they began to die *physically*. But far more important was the *spiritual* death they also experienced. How was this expressed in Genesis 3:21-24?

_____

_____

The effects of this sin and the spiritual death that followed were far-reaching. How did God describe the wickedness of humankind in Genesis 6:5?

_____

Even after the Flood, in which all the wicked were destroyed, what did God conclude about humankind in Genesis 8:21?

_____

Scripture also makes it plain that the sinful nature is not something we obtain by sinning, as did Adam. How did David describe the source of his sinfulness? (Ps. 51:5)

_____

The universal permeation of the earth by sin is also clearly set forth in the New Testament. The most complete teaching on this subject is given in Paul's Epistle to the Romans. In chapter 1 he proves that pagans who have not known the Law of God are wicked and sinful. In chapter 2 he shows that Jews, who have known the Law, are equally sinful and guilty in His sight. And in Romans 3 we see that all people are accountable and guilty before God. In Ephesians 2:3 Paul indicates that we are "by nature objects of wrath."

Practical Applications

In this lesson, you've surveyed the *best* and *worst* about human beings. Every individual is special and significant because he or she is created *in God's image*, with the potential for fellowship with God, and with an eternal destiny. Our worth is ultimately rooted in Genesis 1:26, 27. That worth applies to persons regardless of race, nationality, economic status, or creed. On the other hand, every individual is marred by *sin*. Everyone has a natural inclination for wrongdoing in the form of attitudes and actions. For that reason, no one can enjoy fellowship with his or her Creator except through a relationship with Jesus Christ. To summarize, creation reveals our *significance*, but the Fall reveals our *sinfulness*.

1. Think of a Christian service opportunity you are currently involved in, or that you anticipate involvement in down the road. What impact should the two truths about persons (spoken of above) have on the execution of your ministry?

_____

_____

_____

_____

2. More specifically, how should these truths about persons serve as an impetus for involvement in the ministry of evangelism?

_____

_____

3. For a person who is already a Christian, what practical difference should it make to know that he or she is:

  a) created in God's image?

_____

_____

  b) tainted by a sin nature?

_____

_____

5

THE PERSON
OF CHRIST

The Sunday school teacher asked his group of five-year-olds the following question: "Why did Jesus live on earth?" He wasn't prepared for the profound reply by one of the boys: "God wanted people to know He loved them and some couldn't hear His inside whisper, so He sent Jesus to tell them out loud!"

In his own way, that boy understood the thesis of this lesson: Jesus Christ is the center of the Christian faith. Here's how Paul Little expressed it:

Buddha is not essential to the teaching of Buddhism, or Mohammed to Islam, but everything about Christianity is determined by the person and work of Jesus Christ. Christianity owes its life and character in every detail to Christ. Its teachings are teachings about Him. He was the origin and will be the fulfillment of its hopes. He is the source of its ideas, which were born of what he said and did.
—*Know What and Why You Believe* (Victor Books, p. 59)

Lessons 5 and 6 put the spotlight on the Person and ministry of Jesus. As you delve into these studies, you'll discover what God had in mind when "He sent Jesus to tell them out loud."

His Pre-existence

Jesus did not appear from nowhere on the pages of

47

history, even as the virgin born son of Mary. Rather, as Paul declares, "He is before all things" (Col. 1:17). How is the pre-existence of Jesus primarily seen in John 1:1-17? (Compare Heb. 1:2.)

_____

This revelation takes us back to the very beginning, to the creation itself. How is Christ's pre-existence pictured in I Corinthians 10:4?

_____

Not only does Scripture identify Jesus with the God of the Old Testament, but He is also pictured there as the promised Messiah—the Savior of Israel and the world.

Throughout history the Jewish people have looked forward to the coming of the Christ, their Messiah. What aspect of Christ's life or ministry is prophesied in the following passages?

Isaiah 7:14 _____

Isaiah 53:4, 5 _____

Isaiah 9:7 _____

Jesus Had a Divine as Well as Human Nature

The Bible speaks of our Lord as both the "Son of God," and the "Son of man." These two terms put the spotlight first on the true deity, and then on the true humanity of our Lord. Let's examine what the Bible teaches about the natures of this very unique Person.

His Humanity

It may seem strange that we need to state the obvious: that Jesus was a real human being. But the fact is that people have not always believed it so. In ancient times the Gnostics, who believed that all matter was evil, taught that Jesus only *appeared* to be human. According to the passages below, why is it vital to our faith that Jesus have a truly human nature?

Hebrews 2:14-17 _____

_____

_____

Hebrews 4:14-16 _____

_____

_____

Check out the following reasons for believing this plain and simple truth.

1. Jesus had a human birth—that is, He was born of a human mother. See Matthew 1:18—2:12 and Luke 2:1-20.

Some have argued that since Jesus had a human birth, He must have inherited the same sinful nature as all humans. But this assertion is firmly rejected by Scripture. See II Corinthians 5:21; I John 3:5. What do you think?

_____

_____

2. He grew in childhood and into manhood as a human. From Luke 2:40-52, note down the important facts you find that indicate His growth as a human being.

_____

_____

_____

3. He had many human experiences, such as hunger (Mt. 4:2), sleep (Mt. 8:24), anguish (Lk. 22:44), weariness (Lk. 22:44), and weeping (Jn. 11:35).

What bearing on your Christian life does the fact that Jesus was truly human have?

Hebrews 2:14-17 _____

_____

_____

Hebrews 4:14-16 _____

_____

_____

His Deity

No truth is more important to the Christian faith than is the recognition of Christ's essential nature as deity. Yet the teaching about His deity is so often denied. So let's examine carefully what Scripture really does teach—and be ready to receive it as God's truth.

1. The first indications of the deity of Christ come from Old Testament prophecy. From the following passages, write down those words or phrases that support the belief that Jesus was God come in the flesh.

Isaiah 9:6 _____

Jeremiah 23:5, 6 _____

Micah 5:2 _____

2. The second evidence that Jesus is God is—simply enough, that He said He is! From the following passages, write down first, the statement Jesus made about His deity, and second, the response of the Jews indicating how they *understood* Jesus' statement.

John 5:16-18 _____

_____

John 8:56-59 _____

_____

John 10:30-33 _____

_____

3. The third reason for believing that Jesus is God is that He possesses the qualities of God. What qualities of God are seen in Christ in the following passages?

Matthew 18:20 _____

Matthew 28:20 _____

John 8:58 and 17:5 _____

John 5:21 _____

John 5:26 _____

Hebrews 13:8 _____

4. A fourth reason for affirming the true deity of our Lord is because He performed works that only God could perform. What works of God were performed by Christ in the following passages?

John 1:3; Hebrews 1:10; Colossians 1:16 _____

Colossians 1:17; Hebrews 1:3 _____

Mark 2:5; Luke 7:48 _____

John 6:39; 40; 11:25 _____

John 5:22; II Timothy 4:1; Matthew 25:31-46 _____

_____

In light of the above evidence, we conclude that the claims of Scripture to the full deity of our Lord are strong indeed. The Apostle Paul said of Him that He "is God over all" (Rom. 9:5); "the Lord of glory" (I Cor. 2:8); "in very nature God" (Phil. 2:6); and that "in Christ all the fullness of the Deity lives" (Col. 2:9).

The question is sometimes asked: If Christ was both fully man, and fully God, how could these two natures possibly exist in one Person? If He was but a mere man, this would pose a serious problem. But can we say the same of the God-man? T.C. Hammond (*In Understanding Be Men*) provides us with the commonly accepted Christian position:

1. The two Natures were united but they were not intermingled and altered in their individual properties.

2. There were not transfers of attributes from one to the other, such as a human characteristic transferred to the divine, nor was our Lord's Deity reduced to human limitations.

3. The Union was not an indwelling such as the indwelling of the Christian Spirit of God, but a personal union such that the resulting Being was a Unit, who thought and acted as a Unit.

This brings us to the bottom line in our study. Can we accept Jesus' claims as true? The answer given to this question spells the difference between one who may merely admire certain aspects of Christ's person and ministry and one who accepts His divinity as a true child of God. How does I John 4:1-3 express this truth?

_____

_____

_____

_____

6

THE MINISTRY
OF CHRIST

Its hard to believe some of the things people do in order to gain forgiveness.

A missionary friend once told me of a group of idol worshipers in a foreign country who crawl on their knees for miles toward a sacred temple. Once they reach the foot of the temple steps, they slowly and painfully climb the steps—using only their bare knees—until they reach the idol in the temple. The ritual sometimes takes days to complete, and the peoples' knees are usually scarred and bleeding by the time they reach the idol. This is their way of appeasing their god, of trying to acquire forgiveness for their sins.

Aren't you glad that God doesn't require you to skin your knees in order to be forgiven? Forgiveness of sins is one of the primary benefits *earned for us by Jesus Christ*. Apart from His accomplishments on our behalf, we'd still be padlocked to sin and its eternal consequences. We, too, might resort to crawling on our knees in order to rid ourselves of guilt.

The more familiar we are with the earthly ministry of Christ—particularly His redemptive work on the cross—the more we can appreciate and appropriate benefits such as His forgiveness. Lesson 6 offers a skeletal survey of Jesus' ministry, with emphasis on the significance of His death and resurrection.

Phase One: Beginnings

JESUS' BAPTISM. Jesus' *baptism* you say? Surely He did not need to be baptized—at least not John's kind of baptism. John's baptism had to do with repentance from sin (Mt. 3:11). What reason did Jesus give for His baptism in Matthew 3:13-17?

_____

What do you think Jesus meant by this?

_____

What specific meaning did this event have for John? (Jn. 1:32-34)

_____

JESUS' TEMPTATION. Jesus' baptism was immediately followed by His temptation. Read about this in Matthew 4:1-11. Jesus responded to each of the temptations by:

_____

Compare Satan's approach with his temptation of Eve in Genesis 3:6 and I John 2:15-17. Your observations:

_____

_____

JESUS CALLED HIS DISCIPLES. Following this complete triumph over Satan, Jesus returned to Galilee and began calling His disciples (Mt. 4:18-22). According to the testimony of Jewish leaders of the day, what kind of men did Jesus call? (Acts 4:13)

_____

Let this truth grab your mind for a moment. Remember, these were the men Jesus called "apostles" (Mt. 10:1-4), and sent forth with His full authority into the world. What significance does this fact have for *your* ministry?

_____

EARLY MIRACLES. The first miracle of Jesus is recorded in

John 2:1-11. This miracle is called a _____. It may also be called an "attesting miracle," that is, a supernatural occurrence, the purpose of which is to give proof of Jesus' divine nature and teaching. The effect this miracle had on the disciples was:

_____

What does John say is the purpose of each of the miracles recorded in his gospel? (Jn. 20:31)

_____

Another early example of an attesting miracle is that of the healing of a paralyzed man, in Matthew 9:1-8. In this miracle Jesus first told the man_____.
The Jews reacted _____ . Jesus then healed the paralytic in order to attest that _____

_____.

Matthew 4:23 gives a summary statement of this first phase of Jesus' ministry: *"Jesus went throughout Galilee, teaching in their synagogues, preaching the good news of the kingdom, and healing every disease and sickness among the people."*

Phase Two: Popularity

The second part of Jesus' ministry was marked by great popularity. People came to Him in great crowds, sometimes to hear Him preach, but often, apparently, because of His ministry of miraculous healing. It was during this period that He raised back to life the son of a widow (Lk. 7:11-17), healed the man with a withered hand (Mk. 3:1-6), and performed many other miracles. One of Jesus' great miracles was the feeding of the 5,000. It demonstrated Jesus' creative power as well as His compassion. But Jesus did not always help everyone in need. Why? (See Mt. 13:58.)

_____

Much of Jesus' teaching was given through parables. The word "parable" comes from a Biblical Greek word which means "putting things side by side." Thus, some have described it as "an earthly story with a heavenly meaning." The parable of the sower in Mark 4:1-8 helps us see this meaning more clearly. Read through this parable, then through its interpretation in verses 13-20.

The seed stands for _____;

the birds represent _____;

and the soil _____ .

How does this parable speak to your own heart?

_____

_____

In what ways is it instructive as you consider your ministry to others?

_____

_____

Interestingly, Jesus *gave us* the interpretation of this parable—which is not the case with most parables. Yet His comment in Mark 4:13 may be a hint about how to interpret other parables.

Phase Three: Opposition

The final year of Jesus' ministry was characterized by opposition. It began as Jesus focused attention on His coming suffering and death. As soon as the disciples recognized Him as the Christ, He began to point them to His coming crucifixion and resurrection (Mt. 16:20, 21; Mk. 9:9-12).

During His final week of earthly ministry Jesus was arrested in the Garden of Gethsemane (Mk. 14:43-52); brought to trial before Pilate (Mt. 27:1-31); and crucified (Mt. 27:32-56).

The Significance of the Death of Christ

While the significance of all great men is measured in their contributions in *life*, Christ provided His greatest contribution to the world by His *death*. Four key questions need to be thought through—

Why was Christ's death necessary?
What is the meaning of Christ's death?
What was its value?
What was its scope?

WHY WAS CHRIST'S DEATH NECESSARY? Or *was* it necessary? Some have called it an unforeseen tragedy; or that He died simply because He followed out His own principles, and in this way became an example to us.

Jesus made it perfectly clear, however, that it really was necessary for Him to die. Check Luke 9:20-22 in this regard. Why did Jesus warn His disciples not to tell anyone that He was the Christ?

_____

Two reasons made it necessary for Christ to die:

1. From God's perspective, why was it essential for Christ to die for our sins? (Heb. 2:14)

_____

2. What can we say about mankind that made Christ's death necessary? Scan Romans 1:19—3:20 to find your answer.

_____

WHAT IS THE MEANING OF CHRIST'S DEATH? *The prophet Isaiah seems to give us the heart of the truth when he declares that God shall make His [Christ's] soul an offering for sin (53:10). To understand what that statement means is to understand the atonement.*
—Henry Thiessen, *Lectures in Systematic Theology*

57

Two key words are used to help us understand what happened when Christ died on the Cross. The first of these made particular sense to the Jewish mind; the second to the Gentile mind.

1. His death was the atonement for sin. The Biblical Greek word for atonement, *hilasmos*, speaks of the "means by which sins are forgiven." The parallel Hebrew term was used frequently in the Old Testament. Hebrews 9 and 10 make it plain that Christ's sacrifice was far superior to those of the Old Testament. How is this expressed in Hebrews 9:23-26?

_____

_____

_____

2. Christ's death was a "ransom." The Greek word is *lutron*, meaning "means of release." It was the common word for money used to free slaves. For whom did Christ give Himself as a ransom? (Mt. 20:28; I Tim. 2:6)

_____

WHAT DID CHRIST'S DEATH ACCOMPLISH? Although this topic will be considered in greater detail later, for now notice that:

1. Christ's death satisfied the *justice* of God. The Bible makes it clear that sin results in death (Gen. 2:17; Deut. 24:16, etc.). Our hopeless state, apart from Christ's death, is clearly set forth in Ephesians 2:1-10.

2. Christ's death brought a reconciliation between man and God. This word means to be "put into friendship" with God. See Romans 5:10; II Corinthians 5:18; and Ephesians 2:16 as examples of its use.

WHAT WAS THE SCOPE OF CHRIST'S DEATH? Two different viewpoints are held by Bible scholars. One group emphasizes passages that speak of Christ having died for a limited number of people—for "his people" (Mt. 1:21); "the sheep" (John 10:11, 15); "the Church" (Acts 20:28, Eph. 5:25-27); or for those "chosen" (Rom. 8:32-35).

The other group focuses on those Scripture passages stating that Christ died for "the world" (Jn. 1:29; 3:16); for "all men" (I Tim. 2:6); "for everyone" (Heb. 2:9); and "for the whole world" (I Jn. 2:2).

How do we sort this one out? We start by *accepting both sets of Scripture as true.* Since Paul did not have a problem saying that Christ died for the "chosen" and that He died for "all men," neither should we. Focus your thinking on I Timothy 4:10, then draft your "solution" to this issue, incorporating both aspects of this truth.

_____

_____

_____

What is our responsibility in this area, according to II Corinthians 5:19-21?

_____

_____

The Resurrection of Christ

Although Christ clearly taught that after His death He would rise from the dead (Mt. 16:21; Luke 24:46), the disciples were initially unprepared to accept either His death, or His resurrection. It was only after being reminded by the angels, following the resurrection, that they "remembered his words" (Lk. 24:6, 7).

THE ACCOUNT OF THE RESURRECTION. This account occurs in each of the four Gospels, as well as in many other portions of the New Testament. Read this account now in Matthew 28:1-10. What commission did Jesus give to the two Marys when they met Him on the road?

The other Gospels provide variant readings of this event, evidently incorporating differing parts of the story. Thiessen, in his *Lectures in Systematic Theology*, suggests the following order of this momentous event:

Early that morning three women came to the tomb and saw a vision of angels (Mt. 28:1-8; Mark 16:1-7; Luke 24:1-8). They separated at the tomb, Mary Magdalene going to tell Peter and John (John 20:1, 2), and the other two going to tell the other disciples, who probably were at Bethany (Luke 24:9-11). Then Peter and John ran to the grave ahead of Mary and returned without seeing the Lord (John 20:3-10).

Following this we have twelve appearances of Christ, apparently in this order: To Mary, who came to the tomb after Peter and John had already left it (Mark 16:9; John 20:11-18); to the two on the way to Emmaus (Mark 16:12, 13; Luke 24:13-35); to Simon Peter (Luke 24:34; I Cor. 15:5); to the ten apostles (John 20:19, 24); to more than five hundred brethren at the same time (I Cor. 15:6); to James (I Cor. 15:7); to the disciples on the Mount of Ascension (Luke 24:50, 51; Mark 16:19; Acts 1:9); and to Paul (I Cor. 15:8).

THE IMPORTANCE OF THE RESURRECTION. The major New Testament passage on the importance of the resurrection is I Corinthians 15. In this chapter Paul reviews the Gospel truths which were "of first importance" (vs. 3). What were they?

Some in the church at Corinth rejected the resurrection altogether. What points does Paul make in verses 12-19 to disprove this teaching?

_____

_____

THE RESULTS OF THE RESURRECTION. The resurrection of Christ
is linked to vital Christian truth. Why is the resurrection
important to you?

I Peter 1:3_____

_____

Romans 4:24, 25 _____

_____

Romans 6:4-9; I Cor. 6:14; II Cor. 4:14_____

_____

Ephesians 1:18-23 _____

_____

THE ASCENSION OF CHRIST. The account of the ascension of
Christ to heaven is given in Acts 1:1-11. After reading this
passage, record the main ideas below.

How long did Jesus minister on earth, following His
resurrection? _____

What exciting promise did the angels give?

_____

THE EXALTATION OF CHRIST How is this exaltation described
in Ephesians 1:20, 21?

_____

What is the relationship of Christ's exaltation to the
Church? (Eph. 1:22, 23)

_____

_____

What else did Christ do for the Church following His exaltation? (Eph. 4:7-11)

_____

Describe the *purpose* of these, as given in verses 12-16.

_____

_____

_____

Your Response

Meditate on the words in Psalm 103:1-14. David praised God for His gracious treatment of mankind. You have the privilege of reading these verses from the perspective of the New Testament. The benefits David described accrue to you because of the ministry of Jesus Christ! The gracious character of God, exalted by David, found its ultimate expression in the death of Christ.

As you read, underline the words/phrases in Psalm 103:1-14 that increase your appreciation for Jesus Christ, or refer directly to benefits which His work made possible for you. Then approach the Lord in prayer, giving Him a verbal thank-you note for what He accomplished on your behalf.

7

THE NATURE AND WORK OF THE HOLY SPIRIT

Truths about the Holy Spirit are not always well understood—even by mature Christians. J.O. Sanders testifies:

A preacher was about to deliver a carefully prepared message when there came to him the conviction that it was not appropriate to the group of people before him.

He reluctantly abandoned his manuscript, and seeking the Spirit's guidance, decided to read John, chapter fourteen. As he read, he was alert to discern the message for the occasion. Nor was he disappointed. On reaching verse seven, three words gripped his attention—"Ye know Him"—God the Father. He read two more verses, and a second verse became luminous, "Has thou not known me?"—God the Son. When he reached verse seventeen, a third sentence arrested him, "But ye know Him"— God the Holy Spirit.

These words struck him with tremendous force. Did he really know Him? "I know God the Father," he mused, "and have experienced much of His paternal love and care. I know God the Son, for is He not my Savior with whom I daily commune? But I cannot say that I know the Holy Spirit in any comparable and personal way."

This experience of the author led to a more comprehensive study of the Scriptures relating to the ministry of the Holy Spirit, and resulted in the personal knowledge of Him which had previously been lacking.

—J. O. Sanders, *The Holy Spirit and His Gifts*

How well do *you* know the Holy Spirit? Ask the Lord to use this study on the nature and work of the Holy Spirit to help you come to know Him better—as you have come to know the Father and the Son.

The Nature of the Holy Spirit

HIS PERSONALITY. The question is frequently asked, "Is the Holy Spirit a real person?" "Is he not simply the influence or power of God in the world?" In support of the view that the Holy Spirit is merely a force is the fact that the word for Spirit (*pneuma*) is neuter, rather than—as we might expect—masculine.

But there are at least two solid lines of evidence in Scripture to show that the Holy Spirit is a *person*. The first of these you can find by looking carefully at John 14:17. It is:

_____

See also John 16:8, 13. "He" (*ekeinos*) is a masculine personal pronoun, indicating that the Spirit is a person.

The second evidence that the Holy Spirit is a person rather than a force is affirmed by the personal characteristics ascribed to Him, such as:

Romans 15:30 _____

Ephesians 4:30 _____

Hebrews 10:29 _____

HIS DEITY. We have already studied about *God* the Father and *God* the Son. May we also speak of *God* the Spirit? What relationship between the Holy Spirit and God do you see in the following passages?

I Corinthians 12:4-6 _____

Acts 5:3, 4 _____

We can also see the deity of the Spirit by looking at the works He does, such as:

Job 33:4; Psalm 104:30 _____

II Peter 1:2 _____

John 3:6 _____

Romans 8:11 _____

II Thessalonians 2:13 _____

II Peter 1:21 _____

Scripture also indicates that the Holy Spirit possesses the attributes of God. Some of these are:

Psalm 139:7-12 _____

I Corinthians 2:10, 11 _____

Hebrews 9:14 _____

The Work of the Holy Spirit

IN RELATION TO THE PHYSICAL WORLD. The creation was the work of the Father (Gen. 1:1), through the Son (Jn. 1:3), while the Spirit was possibly the instrument of creation (Gen. 1:2). As Job 33:4 says: "The Spirit of God has made me; the breath of the Almighty gives me life.")

IN RELATION TO SCRIPTURE. What part did the Holy Spirit have in the inspiration of Scripture? (II Pet. 1:21)

_____

Compare also I Peter 1:10, 11; Acts 1:16; Hebrews 3:7; 10:15.

IN RELATION TO CHRIST. What vital part did the Spirit have in the birth of Christ? (See Lk. 1:35; Mt. 1:20)

_____

As Jesus began His ministry He was "anointed" with

the Holy Spirit. (This anointing symbolized His becoming equipped for service.)

For what purpose was Jesus anointed by the Spirit? (Lk. 4:18, 19)

_____

IN RELATION TO SINFUL HUMANKIND. What is the ministry of the Holy Spirit to unbelievers? (Jn. 16:8-11)

_____

After a person is convicted of sin, repents, and receives Christ, the Holy Spirit continues an active role in the life of this new Christian. He brings about the new birth, indwells, baptizes, fills, seals, and gives fruit.

The New Birth

Read John 3, where a very religious and upright man, Nicodemus, conversed with Jesus about religious matters.

What vital principle about becoming a Christian does this passage teach?

_____

How does this passage emphasize the supernatural nature of this experience?

_____

_____

Jesus' words to Nicodemus apply to us as well. Has the Holy Spirit brought this new birth experience into your life? Be prepared to share about this in your group meeting.

_____

_____

_____

_____

If someone asked you what the "new birth" means, how would you explain this Biblical concept to him or her?

_____

_____

The Indwelling of the Spirit

One of the marvelous results of being born into God's family through receiving Christ personally is that the Holy Spirit then comes to reside in our hearts (Gal. 4:6). Is this experience true of all Christians? (Rom. 8:9) Explain.

_____

_____

This fact is made especially clear in I Corinthians 3. The church in Corinth was a long way from what God wanted it to be, as shown in vss. 1-3. Describe their spiritual state, as indicated in these verses.

_____

In spite of the fact that even the "worldly" Corinthians had the Spirit, some people have used Acts 5:32 to prove that the Holy Spirit is not given to all believers. This passage says that the Spirit is given only to

_____

But this verse must be seen in its context. Read verses 27-32. To whom was Peter speaking?

_____

What was their attitude regarding Jesus?

_____

Clearly, if these people would repent and believe, then the Holy Spirit would also be given to them.

Since the Holy Spirit dwells inside of us, what difference should this make in the way we live? Study Acts 1:8

and Ephesians 4:30 before responding.

_____

_____

The Baptism of the Spirit

Before returning to heaven, Jesus promised: "In a few days you will be baptized with the Holy Spirit." The fulfillment of this promise is recorded in Acts 2. This momentous event, accompanied by the disciples being enabled to speak in other languages, was repeated as the Good News extended to the Samaritans (Acts 8:4-17), the Gentiles (Acts 10:44-48), and finally to some disciples of John the Baptist (Acts 19:1-7).

The clearest Biblical statement of what takes place in the baptism of the Spirit is found in I Corinthians 12:12, 13. Bearing in mind that the meaning of baptism is "to place into," describe what happens, according to this passage, when a believer is baptized by the Spirit.

_____

_____

The Filling of the Spirit

The filling of the Spirit is distinct from the baptism of the Spirit. While the baptism of the Spirit takes place once, at conversion, the filling of the Spirit may occur at any time. The verb "be filled" in Ephesians 5:18 is a present imperative—carrying the meaning, "continue being filled" with the Spirit. It indicates that this experience is the intended daily ongoing norm for all Christians.

What practical results of this filling can be seen in the lives of the following people:

The disciples, Acts 4:31

_____

Barnabas, Acts 11:24

Paul, Acts 13:9-12

The Ephesian Christians, Ephesians 5:15-20

Since Scripture commands us to be filled with the Spirit the practical question is: *how?* J. O. Sanders, in *The Holy Spirit and His Gifts*, suggests five practical steps. First, there must be *aspiration*—hungering and thirsting for righteousness (Mt. 5:6). One must keep on asking—as well as seeking, and knocking—for blessing from God (Mt. 7:7, 8). Second, an *acknowledgment* of the lack of this blessing. Third, there needs to be an *abandonment* of sin. Fourth, *abdication* of the "throne" in your heart and placing Christ there instead. Finally, *appropriate* the promise that He will fill us. That is, believe that God keeps His promise, even though you may not feel any differently in your emotions. But as you go about your work for Christ, you will experience a power and blessing that indicates the filling of the Spirit. As He does this, give the praise to God, and to glorify His name for it.

The Seal of the Spirit

Believers in Christ are "sealed" with the Spirit. What does this mean? In ancient times, certain religious groups tattooed their emblems on their followers—called a seal. For a Jew, circumcision was regarded as a seal (Rom. 4:11). *Cruden's Concordance* provides this insight:

Because of the fact that few could read or write, the use of the seal was far more common in olden times than now. Each person had his own private seal which it was a capital crime to copy. This was affixed to every sort of a document, as we now sign our names.

How is the seal of the Holy Spirit described in II Corinthians 1:22?

_____

What is this seal and what does He do? (Eph. 1:13, 14)

_____

_____

The Fruit of the Spirit

The nine-fold fruit of the Spirit found in Galatians 5:22, 23 may be divided into three groups of three.

The first of these: _____, _____, and

_____ is related to *experience*.

The second three _____, _____, and

_____ focus on our *conduct*.

The last three _____, _____, and

_____ have more to do with our *character*.

Having the fruit of the Spirit in our lives is the result of abiding in Christ, as Jesus teaches in John 15. Which aspects of the fruit of the Spirit are most evident in your life?

_____

_____

Where is there need to improve?

_____

The Gifts of the Spirit

Not only was the Holy Spirit given to the Church, but the Church has also been given *gifts* of the Spirit. Three major passages in the New Testament describe these gifts: Romans 12; I Corinthians 12-14; and Ephesians 4. Turn to Romans 12:1-8 and read these verses carefully. What indications do your find that *every* believer has at least one gift?

_____

What attitude are we to have in regard to whatever gifts God has given us?

_____

How can you know which gifts God may have given you? There are three things in this passage which will help you.

First, recognize that all Christians have at least one gift. Probably you have several. Think about yourself with "sober judgment" (vs. 3)—that is, avoid the extremes of either thinking of yourself too highly or too lowly.

Second, since "each member belongs to all the others"— ask other Christians about the gifts you may have been entrusted with. In what ways have they experienced ministry from you?

Third, begin to serve. Ralph Neighbor, in his significant book *This Gift is Mine* says "Christians who stand around waiting for the gifts to appear before they begin to minister never do anything at all." How is this important emphasis taught in vss. 6-8?

_____

Because of time and space limitations, we can only touch on the study of spiritual gifts. Take heart, however! There is another LAMP course devoted entirely to this topic. *How to Discover Your Spiritual Gifts* will help every Christian understand and use his or her gifts in serving Christ.

Wrapping Up

This lesson began with the confession of a gifted and godly servant of God—who confessed that he did not know the Holy Spirit as well as he wanted to. How well do *you* know Him? Take a few minutes now to review this lesson as you answer the following questions:

1. What aspect of the Holy Spirit's personality is most meaningful to you?

_____

2. What aspect of His work is most meaningful to you?

_____

3. In what practical ways can you modify your life-style in order to be more fully used by the Holy Spirit?

_____

_____

4. Identify a particular ministry or service capacity which you often engage in for the Lord.

_____

In what specific ways are you dependent on the Holy Spirit for fruitfulness in this ministry?

_____

_____

5. Whether the realm is Christian living in general, or Christian ministry in particular, how should your dependence on the work of the Holy Spirit reveal itself in your daily life? (To put it another way, how does a person who lives in dependence on the Holy Spirit express that dependence?)

_____

_____

Check your response with Paul's admonition in Ephesians 6:18-20.

8

THE MEANS AND ASSURANCE OF SALVATION

A young adult, guilt-ridden over moral decay in his life, scribbled the following poem.

Sin is real: I feel it flowing in my bloodstream.
Sin is flirty: It keeps vying for my attention.
Sin is smart: It knows when and where to seduce me.
Sin is noisy: I can't turn down the volume.
Sin is alcoholic: It always leaves a hangover.
Sin is strong: It has me pinned to the mat.
Sin is ugly: Looking at it turns my stomach.
Sin is heavy: It has me weighted down.

What is the solution to this young adult's dilemma? What has happened in history that makes a bold escape from the penitentiary of sin possible? What is God's work of salvation on our behalf? What is our response? What assurances of salvation does God's Word offer? As you work through Lesson 8, you'll find answers to those questions.

While salvation needs to be viewed as coming entirely from God—for Scripture makes this entirely plain—nevertheless it is appropriate to speak of our response, as well as God's work, in salvation.

God's Provision of Salvation

Each person in the Godhead has an essential part in bringing salvation to us.

THE FATHER'S PART IN SALVATION. "God so loved the world" is perhaps the single most wonderful truth in all the Bible.

How did God *demonstrate* His love for the world? (See John 3:16 and Romans 5:8.)

_____

_____

Imagine! God loves us so much that He offers us unconditional acceptance! The real challenge of the Christian life is not to try to earn or deserve this love but to accept His offer and believe on His Son.

THE SON'S PART IN SALVATION. The need for a sacrifice for sin can be found throughout the Old Testament. The first such sacrifice was evidently made by God Himself (see Gen. 3:21). This principle of sacrifice is also found in Genesis 4:4 and 8:20. Throughout the Old Testament period, the holiness of God was satisfied only through sacrifices of certain animals.

In the New Testament period, Jesus came specifically to offer His life as the sacrifice for the sins of the world.

How did John the Baptist identify Jesus in John 1:29?

_____

When Christ gave His life on the cross, it was the final, perfect sacrifice for sins forever. See Hebrews 9:24-28; 10:10-14.

The Son's part in salvation was:

_____

_____

THE SPIRIT'S PART IN SALVATION. The principle work of the

Holy Spirit in our salvation is outlined in John 16:8-11. This work is:

_____

_____

What additional work does the Holy Spirit do in connection with salvation? (Jn. 3:1-8)

_____

To help you nail these truths down, summarize the work of the Father, the Son, and the Holy Spirit in salvation, including a key Scripture reference with each.

_____

_____

_____

Our Response to God's Provision

While salvation is entirely God's work, it is our part to respond to God's offer of this free gift: through repentance and trusting Christ personally.

GOD CALLS US TO REPENTANCE. Many people think very lightly about sin—and in many cases may not even realize what sin is. When the Holy Spirit does His work however, things begin to change, leading to repentance. (Note: Repentance means "to change one's mind, or purpose.")

The Bible has a lot to say about the importance of repentance. For example, the message of John the Baptist primarily has to do with repentance (Mt. 3:2). Jesus' ministry began with His message of repentance (Mt. 4:17). Jesus knew that in order for people to come to Him for salvation they must acknowledge the sin and alienation in their lives. Jesus told His disciples that they should preach repentance and forgiveness of sins among all nations (Lk. 24:47). The apostles thus began their preaching ministry by calling on people to repent (Acts 2:38). Paul also said that the first part of his preaching was calling on people to repent (Acts 20:21). Repentance means:

_____

The reason repentance is essential is:

_____

_____

But how can I know if repentance is real? We've all heard of G.I. Joe and his "foxhole religion." He's the guy who "repents" and promises God that if he gets out alive he's going to be different. But when the noise stops and the sky clears, he soon returns to his old ways. Biblical repentance is quite different. It grips a man's whole being: his mind, emotions, and will. Let's draw a bead on these three aspects of repentance.

First, repentance means that the *mind* is alerted to sin. This fact is well illustrated in Luke 15:11-22. Which phrases from this text show that the lost son knew that what he was doing was wrong?

_____

_____

_____

Second, *emotions* are aroused. While emotions vary considerably with individuals, it is difficult to imagine a person whose sense of guilt is not aroused when he is faced with an awareness of sin in his life. How did David express his emotions about his sin in Psalm 38:18?

_____

Scripture makes it plain however, that being sorry for one's sin by itself is not enough. How is this idea brought out in II Corinthians 7:8-10?

_____

_____

Third, the *will* acts. II Corinthians 7 teaches that "godly sorrow" results in action by the will. How is this seen in vs. 11?

_____

_____

How did the Christians in Thessalonica demonstrate their repentance? (I Thess. 1:9)

_____

_____

True repentance involves the _____, the _____, and the _____. In your own words, explain why it is not sufficient for only the mind and emotions to be affected in repentance.

_____

_____

_____

GOD CALLS US TO TRUST CHRIST PERSONALLY. Along with repentance, our need is to receive Christ personally. The offer of salvation is emphasized in varied ways in the New Testament. Check out several of the following passages. John 1:12; 3:16; 4:10; 5:24; Romans 6:23; 10:9, 10; 13; and Revelation 3:20.

Write out a one-sentence explanation of what it means to trust Christ personally.

_____

_____

_____

_____

In John 3:14, 15 Jesus gave a striking illustration of what

77

it means to trust Him personally. This story comes from Numbers 21:4-9 where, because of sin, the children of Israel were dying from poisonous snake bites. When they repented, God instructed Moses to make a bronze snake and place it on a pole. Then, "anyone who is bitten can look at it and live." Read John 3:14, 15 now.

What two great truths about salvation did Jesus point out from this event?

_____

_____

John's Gospel was written so "that you may believe that Jesus is the Christ, the Son of God, and that by believing you may have life in his name" (Jn. 20:31). Throughout this gospel, the life, the miracles and the teaching of Jesus continually testify to who He is and how to receive eternal life through Him.

Our response to salvation is two-fold. These are:

_____

_____

The Assurance of Salvation

A wonderful new life begins when one is born into God's family through faith in Christ. II Corinthians 5:17 tells us that "if anyone is in Christ, he is a new creation; the old has gone, the new has come!" God intends that we rest in the full assurance of this wonderful new relationship. What reasons can we give for having such assurance?

First, look at John 1:12 and 13. To whom does God give the right to become children of God? _____
_____. If you have received Christ, according to this passage, you are born of _____. This means that you now have a spiritual birth—God is now your heavenly Father. What a marvelous truth!

How is this same truth expressed in John 3:16?

_____

_____

_____

In John 3:18? _____

_____

Does God keep His word? If He says that He will give us eternal life, will He do it? _____ On what basis?

_____

_____

John's Bases for Assurance

Just as John's Gospel was written for a particular purpose, so his first epistle was written for another specific purpose. What is that purpose? (I John 5:13)

_____

_____

In I John, five reasons for assurance of salvation are given. Read each of the following passages carefully, then describe the *basis* John gives for assurance of salvation.

I John 2:3-6

_____

_____

I John 2:29; 3:10

_____

_____

I John 3:11-14

_____

_____

I John 3:24b—4:3

_____

_____

I John 5:11, 12

_____

_____

Taking these five reasons as a whole, what is their over-arching thrust? What do they say about the character of true faith?

_____

_____

So What?

An awareness of the means of salvation is important to the saved person as well as the unsaved. Effectiveness in Christian service often hinges on one's capacity to articulate so-called "salvation truths." In what types of ministries is a knowledge of God's plan of salvation most vital?

_____

_____

Check one of the responses to the following statement: "I know how to use my Bible to lead a person to Jesus Christ. I can find at least one reference for each separate truth or step in the plan of salvation." _____ Yes _____ No

If you checked "no," review the content of this lesson, and examine evangelistic tracts used by leaders in your church, until you feel comfortable with the steps involved in leading a person to Christ. Another alternative is to take advantage of any special programs sponsored by your church that offer training in personal evangelism. (A separate _LAMP_ course, _Outreach as a Life-style_ offers special training in the life-style approach to personal evangelism.)

9

THE RESULTS
OF SALVATION

There is an old story about an American Indian who
became a Christian. Sometime after the Indian's conversion the missionary who had led him to Christ visited his
area again. "Tell me" the missionary asked, "how is it now
that you are a Christian?" The Indian replied, "Well, it's
good, but now it feels like there are two dogs inside of me,
a white one and a black one, and they are always fighting."
Feeling that he might be understanding what the native
was saying, the missionary responded: "That's interesting. Which one is winning?" To this the wise old Indian
replied: "The one I feed."

Being able to put into practice some of the things covered in this lesson will depend on which "dog" we feed as
we live out our Christian lives. The greatest apostle of the
Christian faith experienced this struggle even after many
years of devoted service to the Lord: "For what I do is not
the good I want to do; no, the evil I do not want to do—this
I keep on doing" (Rom. 7:19). Other areas are completely
out of our control because of the great work Christ did for
us. These are results of salvation that were "done" for us.

In today's lesson we want to look at what happens when
we make a personal decision to receive Christ. Some of
these results are *positional*—seen from God's perspective.
Others are *practical*—affecting our daily living and actions.

Life Declared Righteous, or Justification

The word "righteousness" means "conforming to the standard, will, or character of God." Paul speaks a great deal about righteousness in his Letter to the Romans. We can't do better than learn from him about this important truth.

After his introduction in 1:1-17, Paul tells us what will *not* bring us into this state of being conformed with God's standard. Let your eye run quickly through Romans 1:18—3:20. Notice that Paul first targets the pagans of his day—the gross sinners if you will, in 1:19-32. Then he picks on those who may have lived fairly upright lives, in 2:1-16. Finally, he takes careful aim at his fellow Jews in 2:17-29.

Summarizing 3:9-18, Paul declares that:

_____

_____

Concerning the possibility of attaining righteousness through keeping the law, Paul makes it plain that (Rom. 3:20)_____

rather, through the law _____.

To get to the heart of Paul's teaching about righteousness, read Romans 3:21-26.

What is its basis from our side?

_____

In what way do we accept it?

_____

In modern times, few of us tend to follow the Jewish law as a means of attaining righteousness. On the other hand, not everyone lives as if they have put complete faith in Jesus Christ who died in our place, taking the punishment we deserve for our sins. What other options do people give today as a basis for being justified by God?

Paul continues this discussion of righteousness in Romans 4, where he teaches that Abraham, the progenitor of the Jewish race, was justified by faith, rather than by works.

What does Paul indicate as the basis for God justifying Abraham in Romans 4:2, 3?

_____

What did Abraham do to have righteousness credited to him? (vss. 18-22)

_____

He then concludes that all people must also be made righteous by faith.

What is the basis for God crediting righteousness to us in vss. 23-25?

_____

_____

_____

Life in the Family of God, or Adoption

The Greek word *huiothesia*, "sonship," was a common word used in the world of Paul's day. According to the *International Standard Bible Encyclopedia*, it was "the legal process by which a man might bring into his family and endow with the status and privilege of a son one who was not by nature his son or his kindred."

Interestingly, this word occurs only in those letters written primarily to Gentile Christians—Romans, Galatians, and Ephesians. These Gentile Christians desperately needed to be assured that they, too, were brought into this special Father-son relationship with God through faith in Christ.

Look now at Romans 8:17. What is one result of our adoption as co-heirs with Christ?

_____

What will be the fuller result of this adoption? (Rom. 8:23)

_____

Combining these two perspectives on adoption, what hope do we as believers have as privileged members of God's family?

_____

Life Transformed, or Sanctification

In justification, God at the beginning of the Christian life declares us acquitted of any wrongdoing. In sanctification, God's will is accomplished as the Christian life proceeds. From Scripture we see that this is a two-sided process. Christians are set apart by God for His use as seen in Hebrews 10:10, "And by that will, we have been made holy [sanctified] through the sacrifice of the body of Jesus Christ once and for all." Thus one aspect of sanctification is that it is a status conferred to believers. Yet the Bible makes it clear that after conversion believers are to grow in a _process_ of becoming more and more sanctified (developing holiness) in daily living. Again the author of Hebrews gives us insight into this second aspect of sanctification. He writes in 12:14, "Make every effort to live in peace with all men, and to be holy [sanctified]; [for] without holiness [sanctity] no one will see the Lord."

In Romans 5—8 Paul teaches us how Christ's righteousness, imparted to us through faith, is to impact our daily living. Reading Romans 5:1-5, list some initial results of this righteousness.

_____

_____

The theme of sanctification continues in Romans. In chapter 6 Paul gives four key words, which, when acted on, will assure that our lives as believers truly are transformed. Beside each of these words, write out the main truth Paul is getting at.

Know (vs. 9) _____

_____

Count (vs. 11) _____

_____

Offer (vs. 13) _____

_____

Obey (vs. 18) _____

_____

In Romans 7 Paul sets forth the truth that living the transformed life can still be a struggle, in spite of all God has done for us in Christ.

How is this struggle summarized—and victory assured? (vss. 24, 25)

_____

_____

In Romans 8 Paul banners the key role of the Holy Spirit in giving us victory over sin. Summarize this role from vss. 5-14.

_____

_____

_____

A discussion of sanctification necessitates examining the fundamental meaning of the Greek word *hagios* (literally, "set apart to, or by, God"), which involves not only separation *from* evil (see I Thess. 4:1-7), but dedication *unto* God as well (see I Pet. 1:15,16; II Pet. 3:11). The word *hagios* is used about 61 times in the New Testament to refer to believers, frequently directed to the establishment of a godly life-style by the believer.

How is the Christian first sanctified? (See I Corinthians 1:2, 30; 6:11.)

_____

_____

This is called *positional* sanctification and occurs when we put our faith in Christ.

A second aspect is called *progressive* sanctification. This means that from a human viewpoint, sanctification is progressive throughout life. How does progressive sanctification involve our decisions and actions? (II Cor. 7:1; Phil. 2:12, 13)

_____

_____

When will the process of sanctification be complete and final? (I Thess. 3:13. Compare also I John 3:2.)

_____

The Trinity is involved in the work of sanctification. The Father sanctifies (I Thess. 5:23) through the offering of Christ (Heb. 10:10) and the agency of the Holy Spirit (I Pet. 1:2).

What *means* does God use for our sanctification?

Hebrews 12:10, 11 _____

John 15:3; 17:17? _____

What difference did God's Word have on Timothy? (II Tim. 3:15)

_____

Life of Fruit Bearing, or Good Works

In John 15 Jesus graphically illustrates the importance and place of good works. Identify:

the true vine _____

the gardener _____

the branches _____.

The key player is the Gardener. What is His objective?

_____

How does He accomplish this?

_____

How is it possible to bear much fruit (vss. 5-8)?

_____

_____

The Relationship of Faith to Works

The Bible speaks clearly about faith *alone* as the means of being justified. In Romans 4 Paul illustrates this truth from the life of Abraham. He backs this assertion with Scripture to irrefutably prove his point. Some sample passages which make this same point are: Matthew 7:23, 24; Romans 3:20; Galatians 2:16; Ephesians 2:8, 9; and Titus 3:4, 5.

Yet the Bible also speaks about how essential works are to the Christian faith. Sample passages include Matthew 5:16 and Hebrews 13:16. In fact, the Book of James especially stresses the key place works have in the life of the Christian. How is this expressed in 2:14-17?

_____

Let your mind grapple with James's statement in verse 18: "Show me your faith without deeds." Do you agree with James's teaching here about the critical importance of works? How would you respond to this challenge?

_____

_____

James uses, of all things, the *same* illustration about Abraham that Paul did, but to prove the *opposite* point! Or does he? Look at 2:20, 21. How did Abraham demonstrate his faith?

_____

According to James, what is the relationship between faith and works? (vss. 22-24)

_____

_____

James then drives his conclusion home: "As the body without the spirit is dead, *so faith without deeds is dead*" (vs. 26).

How shall we deal with this apparent contradiction and disagreement between the teaching of Paul and that of James? Let me suggest this basic difference in viewpoint: Paul was dealing with the *means* of justification; James with the *evidence* for it. The basis clearly is faith and faith alone, apart from the works of the Law, or any other form of work. But just as clearly, works are the evidence of true faith. Action flows from the life we have in Christ just as surely as it flows from the fact that we are physically alive. If we are alive—we move!

In Titus 3:3-8 Paul *balances* these tandem truths. Using your own words, express this truth.

_____

_____

_____

Ephesians 2:8-10 also sets these two Biblical positions in balance. Write these three verses on a small card and consider committing them to memory.

88

Ministry Mandate

One result of salvation, implied by the references dealing with fruit-bearing and good works, should be a life devoted to service in God's Kingdom. Every saved person is "called" into ministry and should view himself or herself as a bona fide "minister" of the Gospel. (**LAMP** has published an entire curriculum of courses to help you become involved in ministry for Christ. See the titles available on the back of this book.) Why did God save us and make us a people for His own possession? "That you may proclaim the excellencies of Him who has called you out of darkness into His marvelous light" (I Pet. 2:9, NASB). In *Body Dynamics* (Victor Books), John MacArthur, Jr. put it this way:

The local church is essentially a training place to equip Christians to carry out their own ministries. Unfortunately, for many Christians the church is a place to go watch professionals perform and to pay the professionals to carry out the church program. In many quarters Christianity has deteriorated into professional "pulpitism" financed by lay spectators. The church hires a staff of ministers to do all the Christian service. This scheme is not only a violation of God's plan, but an absolute detriment to the growth of the church and the vitality of the members of the Body. Every member needs to find a significant place of service. To limit the work of the ministry to a small, select class of full-time clergymen hinders the spiritual growth of God's people, stunts the discipleship process in the Body, and the evangelistic outreach of the church into the community.

Ministries take scores of different forms, and occur in various contexts. Some take place in public, others behind the scenes. Some require formal titles or positions in church programs, others operate informally in the home, neighborhood, or work place. Imagine—whether you're a doctor, lawyer, salesman, mechanic, accountant, or housewife, God wants to use *you* to advance His Kingdom!

If someone asked you the question, "What is your current ministry?" how would you respond?

_____

_____

What service opportunities have you considered getting involved in?

_____

_____

One future possibility is for you to view the contents of this *Truth That Transforms* workbook as a tool for ministry to others. Begin asking God to bring one Christian into your life with whom you could meet on a weekly basis. (Your meetings may not start until you complete this course.) You could obtain a new *Truth That Transforms* workbook, and go over each lesson together when you meet. This ministry role shouldn't be too threatening, since such an informal discipling context doesn't require you to serve as a teacher in a strict formal sense. (If you pursue this ministry alternative, obtain a *Truth That Transforms Leader's Guide* from your church. You can adapt the commentary and group methodologies to a one-to-one situation.)

When you view your completed *Truth That Transforms* workbook as a ministry resource, you're more apt to apply John 15:16: "You did not choose me, but I chose you, and appointed you, that you should go and bear fruit." (NASB)

The name of a person who comes to mind as a prospective study partner is: _____.

10

THE CHRISTIAN CHURCH

As a class exercise, a group of students preparing for the ministry was given the assignment of designing "the ideal church." After receiving large sheets of paper and markers, they were given 25 minutes during class to complete the task. Many immediately began to make architectural drawings, including a large sanctuary, Christian Education wing, and staff offices. Others made lists of activities an ideal church should carry out. One ingenious student drew an enormous building symbolizing all the Christian denominations in the world being unified together. When the time expired, the professor studied each student's work carefully. Finally, shaking his head, he said: "In all your efforts to design the ideal church, *you forgot the people!*"

The word "church" is, of course, used by people in different ways. Some think of it as a denomination, or the hierarchy of a church body. Others think of the whole of Christendom as the Church; others of a building where Christians meet.

When we use the term Church (with a large "C"), we will be talking about the entire body of believers throughout time and throughout the world. This is also known as the Universal Church. And when we use the word church (small "c") we will be talking about a local group of Christians.

The Founding of the Church

The question of when the Church began is an important one, as it relates to what the Church is like, as well as its ministry in the world.

We can learn something important about when the Church began by examining the meaning of the Greek word *ekklesia* in the New Testament. This word comes from *ek*, meaning "from" and *klesis*, "a call." *Ekklesia* was not used exclusively for the Church, however. It was, in fact, commonly used to describe gatherings of people for meetings of any sort. This use of the word is found in Acts 19:41, in connection with the gathering of a riotous crowd who opposed Paul and his mission.

The children of Israel were God's "called out ones." The Hebrew word is *kahal*, derived from a word meaning "to call together." It is regularly translated *ekklesia* in the Greek translation of the Old Testament. Stephen makes reference to this Old Testament "congregation" in Acts 7:38.

The first reference to the Christian *ekklesia* follows Peter's confession in Matthew 16:16, that Jesus was "the Christ, the Son of the living God." In commending Peter, Jesus declares: "On this rock [i.e., Peter's kind of faith and confession] I will build my Church" (Mt. 16:18).

With this background information, describe the similarity as well as the dissimilarity, between Christ's Church and the "church" of the Old Testament:

_____

_____

Between the Christian Church and the secular use of the word *ekklesia*:

_____

_____

Exactly *when* the Church was founded, the New Testament does not tell us. We do know however, that Christ spoke of it as being yet future in Matthew 16:18—"I *will* build my church." The word "church" is first used of a group of believers in Acts 5:11, and following this occurrence, throughout the New Testament. Thus Christ's Church must have been founded some time between when Jesus said it was future, and when we read about it as existing in Acts 5:11.

The coming of the Holy Spirit on the Christians gathered for the Feast of Pentecost in Acts 2 is most frequently pointed to as the time when the Christian Church began.

Looking at Acts 2:4, what was the two-fold effect of the coming of the Holy Spirit on these believers?

_____

With the power of the Spirit upon him, Peter then preached to the assembled crowd, resulting in thousands more being added to the body of believers. The Church has continued growing ever since.

The Nature of the Church

As we have already seen, people have many different ideas about the nature of the Church. To help us understand its true nature, we are going to focus on its spiritual, universal, and local aspects.

THE CHURCH IS SPIRITUAL. We know that the Church is spiritual in nature because:

1. *Entrance* into the Church is by spiritual means. We see this for example, in Peter's sermon at Pentecost. What answer did he give to those who responded to his preaching in Acts 2:38?

_____ and _____.

Baptism here—as it was with John the Baptist—was the outward sign of inward repentance. What does God require for membership in His Church today?

93

Acts 17:30 and II Pet. 3:9

_____

_____

Acts 16:31-33 and Romans 10:9-13

_____

_____

2. *Worship* in the Church is spiritual in nature. As Jesus said in John 4:24, God's true worshipers must worship Him in _____ and in _____.

How are we to worship, according to Philippians 3:3?

_____

(See Rom. 2:28, 29 and Col. 2:11 for "circumcision," referring to true believers.)

How does the apostle Paul urge us to worship God in Romans 12:1?

_____

3. *Growth* of the Church is spiritual in nature. In Colossians 2:6, 7 Paul says that just as we received Christ (by faith), we are to continue to _____ in Him, _____ and _____ in Him.

THE CHURCH IS UNIVERSAL. Although there are hundreds of Christian denominations in the world, the Bible teaches that there is only one true Church.

One of the great experiences I had in visiting Japan many years ago, was to walk into a church service, get down on my knees on their *tatami* mats, and worship God together with fellow Japanese believers. Although I had never met any of them, and could not speak their language, yet I instantly realized that I was part of them, and they of me. We were brothers together, fellow-members of Christ's Church!

This truth is brought out most clearly in Jesus' prayer in

John 17. In verse 11, just before the crucifixion, Jesus prayed "that [the disciples] may be _____." The context helps us understand why Jesus prayed this prayer. In the second half of John 15, and throughout chapter 16, Jesus was preparing His disciples for what was to come. Persecution was near (16:1-3), and He was about to leave them (16:4, 5), for the Cross was at hand, after which they would all be _____ (16:32).

How is this truth illustrated in Romans 12:4, 5?

_____

How is it taught in Galatians 3:28?

_____

Reflect now on this great truth: the Church is one throughout the world. How might this truth affect the way you relate to Christians of other denominations? Of other ethnic backgrounds?

_____

_____

What are some practical ways you can demonstrate the oneness of the Church?

_____

_____

_____

THE CHURCH IS LOCAL. In the early days of the Church in Jerusalem, there was only one local church. Acts 5:11 speaks of "the whole church," and in Acts 8:1 of this church being scattered abroad because of the great persecution that followed the death of Stephen. What did these scattered Christians do, according to Acts 8:4?

_____

As a result, their numbers increased, and soon groups

of believers were meeting in many different places. At first, even these scattered groups of believers were regarded as part of the one Church: "The church throughout Judea, Galilee and Samaria enjoyed a time of peace" (Acts 9:31). Soon however, they became known as separate local churches (see Acts 13:1 and II Cor. 1:1).

Paul's goal, wherever he went on his missionary journeys, was to establish local churches.

What provision did he make for these churches to continue after he left the area in Acts 14:23?

_____

Paul's purpose was to organize a church in every place where there was a group of believers. This purpose is further demonstrated in such passages as I Corinthians 1:2; Philippians 1:1, and I Thessalonians 1:1. From these passages we clearly see that Paul *did* establish churches throughout his journeys.

The Ministry of the Church

Sometimes people think or ask the question: "What is the Church here for anyway?" It is a legitimate question. To begin answering, let's go back to the very first Church. When it was founded the Holy Spirit immediately came upon the believers. What did their ministry as a church consist of? Surely their example is a key to what the Church should be doing today.

According to Acts 2:42, four key aspects of the early church's ministry included:

_____

_____

THE MINISTRY OF TEACHING. The teaching ministry of the apostles was crucial to the survival and growth of this little band of followers of the Christ. What was it that the apostles were teaching? (Compare Matthew 28:20.)

Study the elements of Peter's first "sermon" on the day of Pentecost (Acts 2:36-39). List some of the key points Peter used to lead those unbelievers in Jerusalem to a saving knowledge of Christ.

What is the source of this teaching today? (II Tim. 3:16)

What is its goal? (II Tim. 3:17)

A teaching ministry doesn't always have to be a formal affair in a classroom with 20 or more students. List some ways you could be involved in your church's teaching ministry, whether formal or unstructured.

THE MINISTRY OF FELLOWSHIP. As it was in the days of the New Testament, fellowship continues to be a critical need among Christians today. Turn to I John 1 and read the first seven verses. Looking at this passage carefully, what is the *basis* for our fellowship?

What is the *condition* for continued fellowship?

At the time of this writing our church has almost 1,000 attenders and 3 services on Sunday morning. Unless your church is the size of the pre-Pentecost Jerusalem congregation (see Acts 1:15), you may find fellowship difficult.

What are some strategic ways today's church members can maintain the ministry of fellowship?

_____

_____

THE MINISTRY OF WORSHIP. The breaking of bread for these early Christians was a vital part of their worship. The focus of it was on the death of Jesus Christ for their sins and their life because of union with Him. Worship has always been central in God's plan for His people.

Jesus summarized all the commands in the Old Testament into two. The first of these was: (Mk. 12:29-30)

_____

As you reflect on the worship at your church remember that worship is *not* based on how well the pastor preaches or the choir sings. Worship begins and continues as each person in the pew directs his or her attention to expressing love to God through the various aspects of the service. Are you content with the worship in your church? Or should the question be, "Are you content with the worship of God in your heart?"

List two ways you can better prepare yourself for worshiping God by Sunday of this next week.

_____

_____

THE MINISTRY OF PRAYER. Finally, the earliest Christians gave themselves to united prayer.

What promises does Jesus make to those who pray together? (Mt. 18:19, 20)

_____

How would you describe the kind of praying Paul urges in Ephesians 5:18?

_____

For what was the Corinthian Church urged to pray, in II Corinthians 1:8-11?

It has been said that the popularity of a *church* is measured by its Sunday morning attendance; the popularity of the *preacher* by its Sunday evening attendance; but the popularity of the *Lord* is measured at the prayer meeting. What opportunities are available in your church to pray as a body? What has been your attitude toward this absolutely essential ministry of the Church?

The Mission of the Church

What God has called the Church to do in the world is clearly set forth by Jesus in Matthew 28:18-20. The central command of this passage is "make disciples." Everything else in verse 19 is supportive to that task. Thus, the participles that follow support the command to make disciples. "Going," "baptizing," and "teaching" tell us *how* the task of making disciples is to be carried out.

Going implies that the Church will have a ministry of outreach. Each local church should have a vision, as well as an action plan, to carry the Good News effectively into its community.

How was this command carried out by the church at Thessalonica? (I Thess. 1:7, 8)

Speculate, if you will, as to who was included among the Thessalonians, in this glowing report by Paul.

Baptizing tells us that the result of that witness to the community will be that some will respond to the message, receive Christ, and be baptized. We are to expect *fruit* from our witness.

The third participle, *teaching*—the kind Jesus is refer-

99

ring to—is where churches frequently fail. What does this verse tell us about the *quality* of this teaching?

While many churches teach a great deal concerning Biblical truth, one minor word seems to be woefully lacking when it comes to carrying out the truths taught in Scripture. Search Matthew 28:20 again, carefully, to determine the difference between *quality* teaching and just imparting facts.

The result of this teaching is obvious: we have equipped believers for service. They in turn are now ready to go, to evangelize and train others. The cycle is thus—and only because of this step—made complete.

What is Jesus' promise as we go on obeying Him? (vs20)

This training ministry by the church is also the focus of Paul's teaching in Ephesians 4. What is the primary task of leadership, according to verse 12?

What are some of the results of this ministry, according to verses 13-16?

Equipping Station

If the primary function of local church leaders is to equip laypeople for their ministries, then the responsibility (and privilege!) of members of a congregation is to avail themselves of training opportunities.

What ministry training opportunities does your church frequently sponsor? (If necessary, call a staff member and inquire about opportunities slated for the next six months.

Add those items to your answer.) Possibilities may include teacher training seminars, evangelism classes, and training in specialized opportunities such as jail ministry, peer counseling, and so forth. Jot down training opportunities that periodically show up on your church's calendar. You may also list training events periodically scheduled by Christian colleges or parachurch organizations in your area.

_____

_____

_____

_____

_____

_____

Put an asterisk beside those training opportunities that you have already experienced. Next, circle one of the training events that you feel God is nudging you to attend in the future, which you feel would enhance your ability to help the church fulfill its mission.

If you aren't aware of practical training opportunities in an area for which you're burdened, broach your need to a member of the pastoral staff. Inquire about the feasibility of future training in this area.

Note: Other courses in this series are specifically designed to help churches equip their people for ministry. A brief listing of courses in this curriculum may be found on the back cover of this book. You may also write or call *LAMP* for further information about courses that can help your church more effectively fulfill the Great Commission.

11

THE SPIRIT BEINGS

When it comes to the subject of "spiritual beings"—angels, demons, and Satan—folks often tend to go to one of two extremes. Some people scoff at the idea of spiritual beings, citing the irrationality of believing in their existence; some align themselves with supernatural forces in an unwise and unbiblical fashion.

Evidence of the second reaction abounds. Back in the 1970s, when Doubleday publishers opened a new book club of occult titles, membership zoomed to 100,000 in two years. Anton LaVey, priest of the Church of Satan, in San Francisco, often "blesses" the congregation with the following words: "May all your lustful thoughts reach fruition. Hail Satan!" In Norman, Oklahoma, it was reported that members of a secret teenage fraternity adopted the name "Covenant of the 73rd Demon." Members vandalized church property—ripping Bibles apart, turning crosses upside down, etc.—to prove their loyalty to the devil.

Many seem to rely on TV programs such as "Highway to Heaven" to inform them about angels, and movies such as "The Exorcist," "Ghostbusters," and "Ghoulies" to teach them about demons or Satan. Instead, let's consult a more reliable source: God's Word. Lesson 11 surveys what the Bible says about these spiritual beings, and tells why awareness of their existence is important.

Teaching About Angels

THE ORIGIN OF ANGELS. The Bible may not tell us everything
we want to know about angels but it does tell us plainly
that there *are* angels. Jesus clearly believed in them (Mt.
13:32; 8:38; Mk. 13:32; 8:38;), as did the apostles (Jn. 1:51;
I Pet. 3:22; Heb. 12:22).

What indication is there that angels are *created* beings?
(Col. 1:16, 17)

_____

What does Psalm 148:2-5 suggest as to the *time* of their
creation?

_____

What does Hebrews 12:22 tell us about their *number*?

_____

THE NATURE OF ANGELS. The primary character of angels is
indicated by the name "holy" given to them.

What hint do we have about their gender? (Mt. 22:30)

_____

What else can we learn about them? (II Thess. 1:7;
II Pet. 2:11)

_____

What about their length of life? (Lk. 20:35, 36)

_____

THE ABODE OF ANGELS. Where do angels generally dwell?
(Mt. 18:10 and 24:36)

_____

Where is their place of ministry? (Heb. 1:14)

_____

THE WORK OF ANGELS. Of the 273 references to angels in the
Bible, most speak of their ministry, or work. For example,

angels are seen to:

Psalm 148:1, 2 _____

Acts 8:26 _____

Psalm 91:11, 12 _____

Acts 12:23 and Revelation 16:1-12 _____

THE FUTURE OF ANGELS. The only hint we have about angels' future is found in Revelation 21:10-14. What does this passage tell us about their future?

_____

MINISTERING TO US! Angels are described as "ministering spirits sent to serve those who will inherit salvation" (Heb. 1:14).

I will never forget the time I was pulling a grain binder down a steep hill and lost control. As the massive tractor and binder churned down a deep ditch "something" said clearly to me: "You had better get off." Unknown to me, a driveway blocked the ditch just ahead. Completely relaxed, I dropped off into the side of the ditch. Had I gotten off a split second later I would have taken to the air, over the top of the tractor. Had I gotten off a second earlier, the binder would have ground my prostrate body to death. What was that "something" that told me to get off at that precise moment? One of God's angels was evidently ministering to me in that moment of dire need.

Angels minister to those who will inherit salvation. Perhaps you, too, have a story to tell, when you experienced the special protection or presence of God. Note it below, and be prepared to share it during your group discussion.

_____

_____

_____

Teaching About Demons

THE ORIGIN OF EVIL ANGELS. Our study of angels showed that they were created by God. But since God cannot create evil, we are left with the problem of how demons came into existence. What hint as to their sinful origin can you find in Jude 6?

_____

THE NATURE OF EVIL ANGELS. What information about a demon's nature can you find in the following passages?

Matthew 10:1; 12:43 and Mark 1:23-26 _____

Mark 1:21-28 _____

James 2:19 _____

Ephesians 6:12 implies a hierarchy of evil spiritual forces who are opposing the work of God. According to the context of this passage (vss. 10-18) how can we gain victory over these warring spiritual forces?

_____

_____

_____

THE PLACE OF EVIL ANGELS. Just as the holy angels have their abode with God, so the evil angels have their abode with Satan (compare Rev. 12:7-9). Where are the evil angels usually found (Eph. 2:2)?

_____

Where else are they found (Eph. 6:18)?

_____

THE WORK OF EVIL ANGELS. The work of demons is seen throughout the gospels, causing such things as blindness (Mt. 12:22) and deafness (Mt. 9:32, 33); indwelling people

(Mt. 8:28-34); and motivating fortune-telling (Acts 16:16-18). But there is more. How is the activity of demons seen in I Timothy 4:1?

_____

Looking at the context of this verse, how is the Christian to respond to these evil influences?

_____

THE FUTURE OF EVIL ANGELS. What future awaits the fallen angels according to Jude 6?

_____

Teaching About Satan

THE ORIGIN OF SATAN. As with the angels, the origin of Satan is not clearly revealed. The "serpent" in the Garden of Eden was the devil (Rev. 12:9 and 20:2). But where did he come from?

Isaiah 14 is a prophecy against Babylon, and Ezekiel 28 is a prophecy against the King of Tyre. Yet many Bible scholars believe that these prophecies also refer to Satan and reveal his origin. If so, what does Ezekiel 28:11-19 teach about:

His original position (vs. 14) _____

_____

His original nature (vss. 12 and 15) _____

_____

His sin, or reason for his fall (vss. 16, 17)_____

_____

The results of his sin (vs. 16) _____

_____

Now read Isaiah 14:12-15 and state the basic reason for

Satan's fall: _____

_____

The original sin—the sin of Satan himself—is thus revealed as the sin of pride. With the words "I will . . ." Satan rears up to challenge his Maker. Pride is the original sin; the great sin. Examine your own heart now, just as I am examining mine. Pride is claiming for ourselves that honor which is due only to God. Does it still destroy God's work today? We know that it does. Let us recognize pride's ugly Satanic head and call it what it is: *sin*. Let us rather give all that we are, all that we can ever be or do, and with it place ourselves at His feet in an act of worship. In so doing we acknowledge that all things are of Him and through Him. He alone is worthy. Worthy is the Lamb of God!

THE NATURE OF SATAN. How is his nature or character described in:

Matthew 3:19 _____

I Thessalonians 3:5 _____

Satan's character is aptly described in I Peter 5:8. It is:

_____

In Revelation 9:11 he is called Abaddon (meaning "destruction") and Apollyon (meaning "destroyer"). This tells us a lot about his character and purpose in the world!

THE ABODE OF SATAN. Because Satan is a spirit being, he can, as do angels and demons, travel anywhere. Where is the main place of Satan's activity? (Job 1:7)

_____

THE WORK OF SATAN. Satan can and does:

Matthew 13:36-40 _____

Matthew 4:1-9 _____

II Corinthians 2:5-11 _____

II Corinthians 4:4 _____

II Corinthians 11:13-15 _____

II Timothy 2:26 _____

THE FUTURE OF SATAN. The Bible leaves us with no doubt as to the destiny of Satan.

_____

When did Satan's judgment really begin? (Gen. 3:14, 15)

_____

What were the two results of Christ's death on the cross, according to John 12:31-33?

_____

What is the place and nature of his final judgment? (Rev. 20:9, 10. Compare also Mt. 25:41)

_____

Battle Readiness

Though we don't want to underestimate the power of Satan, this lesson shouldn't inject a pessimistic, defeatist attitude into our minds. Even now, before the final judgment when Satan's power is totally cut off, we can experience victory over him. Our Commander-in-Chief has provided weapons of warfare to help us in the battles. In our daily struggles against Satan, we aren't left to our own meager resources. Paul encouraged the Corinthians with these words: "For though we live in the world, we do not wage war as the world does. The weapons we fight with are not the weapons of the world. On the contrary, they have divine power to demolish strongholds" (II Cor. 10:3, 4).

What "weapons of warfare" do the following references mention?

Colossians 4:2-4 _____

II Timothy 3:16, 17 _____

Hebrews 10:24, 25 _____

Which of the weapons of warfare do you most often neglect? Realistically, what can you do in this area to better prepare yourself for the inevitable daily warfare with Satan?

_____

_____

_____

_____

12

THE LAST THINGS

Since the earliest days of the Christian church, eschatology (the study of "last things") has aroused both curiosity and speculation. Occasionally, an individual has even set a specific date for "end time" developments. For example, a booklet predicting the rapture of the Church in the autumn of 1988 sold hundreds of thousands of copies. And as the proposed deadline neared, the author purchased a vacation home with the profits!

Back in the 1970s, a pastor in Chicago produced a 13 minute videotape titled, "Millions Are Missing." The tape begins, "This is a chaotic and confusing time. Millions of people have mysteriously disappeared, and I am one of them." According to an article in the *Los Angeles Times*, the pastor delivered the tape to the three major TV networks, to be played after the rapture of the church for the benefit of persons left behind.

Ironically, the fact that eschatology is subject to vain speculations and excessive preoccupation reveals its importance to believers. An unimportant topic wouldn't receive such attention. What does Scripture teach about Christ's return and related events? What difference should our awareness of His return make in our lives *now*? What different interpretive frameworks have Christians held throughout history? For answers, complete the workbook assignments that follow. Lesson 12 won't resolve all the questions folks have about the end times, but it does provide some basic information to serve as a catalyst for your thinking.

The Return of Christ

THE FACT OF CHRIST'S RETURN. Most doctrinal statements and creeds of the various church bodies affirm their faith in the return of Christ. These statements are based solidly upon statements Jesus made that He *would* come again, such as those in Matthew 16:27; 26:64; John 14:1-3; 21:21-23, as well as through the message of a heavenly angel in Acts 1:11.

THE TIME OF HIS RETURN. Lots of religious groups have gotten into difficulty setting dates about the time of His return. But Jesus clearly stated: "No one knows about that day or hour" (Mt. 24:36).

Yet the Bible does say certain things about the time of His return, which we will look at now. In I Thessalonians Paul addressed the question of the timing of Christ's return because many were concerned about Christians who had died (4:13). What information about the time of His return can you gather from I Thessalonians 5:1-3?

_____

_____

This question is again addressed by Paul in II Thessalonians 2. What event must precede the coming of Christ, according to vss. 1-4?

_____

THE SIGNS OF HIS RETURN. In Matthew 24:3 the disciples asked Jesus: "What will be the sign of your coming and of the end of the age?" Read verses 3-14 and describe the world situation at that time:

Religiously _____

_____

Politically _____

_____

Economically _____

_____

How then should we live? Jesus brings this discussion to
a practical conclusion in Matthew 25 with three parables.
Read each of these parables and state the main thrust you
understand Jesus to be making.

The parable of the ten virgins, 25:1-13.

_____

_____

The parable of the talents, 25:14-30.

_____

_____

The parable of the sheep and the goats, 25:31-46.

_____

_____

How do these applications compare with Paul's in I
Thessalonians 5:4-11?

_____

The Resurrection

Although not everyone in the New Testament period

believed in the resurrection—such as the Sadducees—
Jesus settled this issue for all time in Matthew 22:23-33. In
this passage He says that since Abraham, Isaac, and Jacob
are *alive*, there is a resurrection (in which they will participate). Compare also Luke 20:37.

The most detailed information on the resurrection of
the believer is given in I Corinthians 15. Let's examine this
passage carefully.

How does Paul emphasize the importance of the resurrection in verses 12-19?

_____

At what time will the resurrection take place (vs. 23)?

_____

After examining verses 35-49, briefly describe the body
Christians will have following the resurrection.

_____

_____

Now let's look at another passage. According to Jesus
(Jn. 5:28-30), what two groups of people will arise? With
what results?

_____

_____

This would be a good passage to share with a friend
who might be wondering about life after death.

The Judgments

Jesus taught in John 5:28-30 that two groups of people
will arise to be judged. Who are they and what will be the
difference in their judgment? You may also compare
Revelation 20:4-6 and 20:11-15.

_____

_____

THE JUDGMENT OF BELIEVERS. This judgment is spoken of most clearly in I Corinthians 3. The church at Corinth was plagued by worldliness and sin, verses 1-3. In verses 10-15 Paul describes what the judgment of believers will be like. What in this passage indicates this as the judgment of believers?

_____

What is Paul indicating by the picture of "gold, silver, and costly stones"?

_____

By "wood, hay and straw"?

_____

Why is it important to make it our goal to please God? (II Cor. 5:10)?

_____

_____

THE JUDGMENT OF UNBELIEVERS. We have already learned that unbelievers will also be raised from the dead.

On what basis will they be judged (Rev. 20:11-15)?

_____

The Reign of Christ

The Scripture on this subject has been understood by Christians in different ways, with interpretations of end-time events described as *Premillennialism, Postmillennialism*, and *Amillennialism*.

Premillennialists believe that Christ will come suddenly, and will set up His kingdom in Jerusalem, from whence He will rule in holiness and righteousness for a 1000 years (a literal millennium). Christians will reign with Him. This period which will be followed by a final rebellion of Satan, his judgment (along with that of all unbelievers), and the ushering in of an eternal state of righteousness (the new heaven and earth).

Postmillennialists on the other hand, believe that the Kingdom of Christ will grow gradually during this present age until a period of great prosperity and blessing for the Church (the millennium, but not necessarily a literal 1000 years) is ushered in. At the close of this period wickedness will again dominate the earth, to be followed by Christ's return to set up an eternal reign of righteousness.

Finally, *Amillennialists* believe that the 1000 years spoken of in Revelation 20 is symbolic of a long period of time. Thus there is probably no *literal* reign of Christ on earth. Rather, Christ's "reign" is in the hearts and lives of His people in every age, as well as with all Christians who have died and gone to heaven. The present age will end with the coming of Christ, the resurrection, and the judgment of the dead, followed by a state where God reigns and rules eternally.

Amazing! True Christians, all believing the same Bible, see these truths differently. The basic reason for this is because not all Christians hold to the same *principles* of interpreting Scripture. Awareness of this fact should help us in two ways: 1) to recognize that Scripture passages related to this subject are capable of more than one interpretation; and 2) to be charitable toward those holding to interpretations differing from our own.

A. A. Hodge tells us that the Premillennial view "prevailed generally throughout the Church from A.D. 150-250." After about A.D. 250 however, Christian leaders began to think of the Church more in terms of a visible empire reigning over pagan empires and started interpreting Scripture from a *Postmillennial* view—which held sway in the church for many centuries. The Reformation brought a return to the *Premillennial* and the *Amillennial* views.

Many evangelicals believe that the *Premillennial* view is correct for the following reasons:

1. It calls for a more literal interpretation of the Old Testament prophecies regarding the future kingdom. (See Isaiah 2:1-4 and 11.)

2. It sees Christ as reigning on earth, in accord with Old Testament passages that seem to indicate such a situation: Jeremiah 23:5, 6; Micah 5:2 and Zechariah 14:8, 9.

3. It provides for the restoration of the earth to at least its state before the curse. Compare Romans 11:25-28.

4. It provides a future for the people of Israel. Compare Romans 11:25-28.

On the other hand, many other Christians are *Amillennialists* and point to the following reasons for their position:

1. The New Testament sometimes interprets the Old in a symbolical sense. For example, Jesus did this with His words about Elijah in Matthew 17:11-13. See also Galatians 4:24 and I Peter 3:21. Some say this symbolical approach should be used in interpreting Old Testament prophecies regarding the coming Messiah.

2. The Book of Revelation is a symbolical book, and therefore Revelation 20 should not be taken literally in regard to the millennium.

With world events since World War I (the world does not appear to be getting better and better), a declining number of Bible students hold the *Postmillennialist* position.

With which of these views are you most comfortable? Why? Does your church encourage a particular view of the end time? Of what practical value does your position hold for Christian living today?

_____

_____

_____

_____

_____

_____

_____

The Future in Present Tense

God wants us to understand how truths about last things should affect our lives in the here-and-now. Many Bible passages that mention Jesus' return or related events also give commands about how we should live *now* in the light of those future realities. Examine the following references. Record words and phrases from each passage which point to attitudes, actions, or character qualities that should describe us *now*.

1. II Corinthians 5:1-11

_____

_____

2. I Thessalonians 4:13—5:11

_____

_____

3. II Peter 3:1-18

_____

_____

4. II Peter 3:1-18

_____

_____

5. James 5:7-11

_____

_____

In view of these passages, one change in your habit patterns, schedule, or character that the Holy Spirit is showing you a need for is:

_____

_____

LESSON PLANS

Welcome to the challenging privilege of leading a Lay Action Ministry Program (LAMP) study group! *Truth that Transforms: A Study in Christian Doctrine* is one in a series of LAMP courses that strive to equip laypersons as ministers in the church and in the world. Throughout this course, by your enthusiasm for the subject matter and thoroughness of preparation, you will be able to model the kind of commitment to ministry that you want your group participants to adopt.

To prepare for each group session, examine the workbook lesson thoroughly. Your own completed workbook exercises will increase your sense of poise as you lead and will provide a basis for supplementing insights shared by group members. Though your primary role will be to facilitate discussion of Bible study assignments and their application, you will often need to provide input of your own.

The next phase of preparation is to review the lesson plan in this Leader's Guide. Based on variables such as characteristics of your learners, time limitation, meeting place, and your experience as a teacher, you will need to adapt each week's suggestions to fit your particular situation. View the suggested procedures as a guide for exploring the lesson theme, not as a straitjacket which restricts your freedom as a teacher.

Important Notes

• Concerning the use of workbook assignments in group meetings: When members of a study group meet to go over workbook assignments, a common procedure is to cover each question or phrase in consecutive order, asking for verbal feedback on each item. That approach isn't always necessary, however, because of the clear-cut answers to some questions. Furthermore, such methodology can quickly become tedious and may fail to stimulate further thought on the workbook content.

Throughout this Leader's Guide, you'll find activities and questions which allow learners to draw from their homework assignments without necessarily covering every single item. Occasionally, you'll be instructed to cover selected workbook activities verbatim. At other times, you'll ask questions or give "in class" assignments not provided in the workbook. You want to cover lesson concepts as creatively and meaningfully as possible.

However, also avoid the extreme of seldom allowing learners to share workbook material. To work hard on assignments without receiving an opportunity to share findings or hear the fruit of others' study is frustrating and demotivating. Even when lesson plan instructions do not ask you to do so, give participants an opportunity to ask questions about assignments which they found difficult or confusing.

• Concerning questions provided in the lesson plans: Each lesson plan offers a skeletal outline of a way to structure your class time from start to finish. Though a variety of methodologies are recommended, the most common tool provided for your use as a teacher is questions. Your weekly preparation should include writing out your answers to each question in the lesson plan (the questions usually aren't the same as study questions provided in the workbook). The lesson plan questions will force you to review, to synthesize, and to apply workbook content in advance of the group meeting. This preparation strategy will free you to concentrate on the group members and their needs as you proceed through a lesson.

• Concerning an Introductory Group Meeting: Preceding Lesson 1, schedule an Introductory Meeting of your study group. Distribute the Truth that Transforms workbooks; introduce the distinctives of a LAMP study course; emphasize the prerequisite of weekly assignments; become acquainted with one another as persons; and pray together for the Holy Spirit's work in and through course participants.

• Concerning the atmosphere of the group meetings: The cultivation of meaningful relationships among group members is integral to the success of the course. Incorporate key ingredients for healthy group life into each session: mutual accountability for application; personal sharing of struggles as well as victories related to the task of service in the church; and intercessory prayer.

As you contemplate the responsibility of group leadership, allow the words of I Corinthians 15:58 to encourage you: "Stand firm. Let nothing move you. Always give yourselves fully to the work of the Lord, because you know that your labor in the Lord is not in vain."

Lesson 1

FOCUS: Let several volunteers respond to this opening question: Why is it important to study what the Bible says about God, anyway? After several minutes, interject the following quote from the late A. W. Tozer: "What we believe about God is the most important thing about us." Now ask for additional comments or personal illustrations based on Tozer's quote.

Wrap-up the introductory focus time by making a few brief statements to the effect that our belief or lack of it inevitably translates itself into our actions and attitudes.

DISCOVER: To cover the "Existence of God" section:

First ask: What position or perspective do Bible authors take concerning the existence of God?

Instruct your learners to skim several Psalms not mentioned in the workbook: Psalm 8; 33:6-12; 65:5-13; and 104. Based on input from these passages, discuss: What specific attributes of God are revealed in His creation? (Majesty, strength, wisdom, creativity, etc.)

To cover "The Nature of God" section, give group members an opportunity to use their completed assignments as a basis for responding to the following questions:

1. What new or fresh insight about God did you uncover in your study?

2. In your opinion, which truth about God provided the most encouraging insight? Why? The most convicting insight? Why?

3. Which truth about God do you think is least recognized or appreciated by Christians today? Why do you think this is the case?

4. Which name of God is most meaningful to you? Why?

5. On which questions in this workbook section are you the most eager to hear the written responses of other group members? (Take time for interaction at this point in the lesson. Be particularly sensitive to persons who are unsure of an answer they jotted down, and need clarification.)

DISCUSS: Refer participants to John 4:24 and Psalm 100. Ask:

1. What are some logical human responses to the characteristics of God we're covering?

2. How can parents of young children use elements of creation as spontaneous teaching aids?

3. What are some illustrations of ways you have used nature to teach another person or child about God?

RESPOND: A logical reaction to the introductory material

about God in this lesson is to participate as a group in corporate expressions of worship. Employ one or both of the following suggestions:

(a) Ask for a couple of brief testimonies that relate to one of the content elements covered in the lesson. For instance, someone could share about a time when God's presence and reality was made clearer through an encounter with nature. Or another could tell how God provided for a material need as a means of illustrating one of His names (for example, Jehovah-Jireh, "the Lord will provide.")

(b) Use a record or cassette tape to play a worshipful song, the lyrics of which relate to the content of the lesson. ("How Great Thou Art," "Master Designer," and "This Is My Father's World" are possibilities.) Or sing choruses together that elevate the Person of God ("God is So Good," etc.)

Lesson 2

Focus: Ask: How does another person get to know you intimately?

After acknowledging responses, emphasize the necessity of personal revelation. (No one can know us intimately unless we reveal information about ourselves.) Use this discussion about personal revelation to broach the subject of knowing God. Explain that religions other than Christianity began with some human attempt to discover or explain God. But Christianity depends on God's revelation of Himself! God took the initiative. Without this deliberate Divine revelation, we'd be in the dark concerning Him. Point out that this second lesson on God the Father takes an even closer look at what He has revealed about Himself in the Bible.

Discover: To cover the concept of "Trinity" ask learners to review their completed workbook assignments as a basis for responding to the following questions:

1. Which Scripture reference most convincingly shows that the Father is God? That Jesus is God? That the Holy Spirit is God?

2. Which illustration used by the author do you find most helpful in illuminating this concept?

3. Why is acceptance of God as a Trinity an important doctrine?

To cover the workbook section on "The Attributes of God," give participants a few minutes to review their completed assignments, then ask:

1. Which divine attribute is most meaningful to you personally at this stage in your Christian experience? Why?

2. Regarding which workbook exercise or attribute do you most need or want to hear the written responses of others in the group? (Asking this type of question prevents the monotony of reviewing every single Bible study exercise, yet allows learners to deepen their own findings in areas of need or confusion. The goal is to create an environment of cooperative learning.)

DISCUSS: Next, divide into groups of three or four persons. Give members of each small group ample time to brainstorm answers to the following question: What are some practical implications of each divine attribute for our daily lives?

Point out that individuals may already have a few responses jotted down in response to application-oriented workbook questions. By working together, they can expand the list of applications for each attribute. (To make sure all the attributes are covered in the limited amount of time you have, instruct half the groups to work backwards through the list of attributes, beginning with God is Good," while the other groups begin with the first attribute listed, which is "Eternal.")

After about twelve minutes, call a halt to the brain-storming activity. Ask a representative from each small group to share aloud just two of the practical implications they listed. As each representative shares, encourage other participants to add contributions from their notes.

RESPOND: First, let volunteers share their responses to the three questions in the workbook section labeled "What This Means To Me." Use this time as an additional opportunity to show, through personal experiences of group members, the practicality of comprehending divine attributes.

Second, direct everyone to select one attribute in this lesson, and to think of a way to share its meaning (and practical implications) with another person or group before the next session.

Lesson 3

FOCUS: Refer your learners to the anecdote about Billy Graham in the introduction to Lesson 3 of the workbook. Discuss: What difference did Graham's renewed confidence in Scripture make in his ministry? What is the relationship between one's confidence in Scripture and his or her motivation for obedience and Christian ministry?

To provide transition, emphasize that lesson content, drawn from the Bible, should deepen our confidence in Scripture and further equip us to use it in ministry endeavors.

DISCOVER/DISCUSS: First, take several minutes to review the three possible sources for Christian living and doctrine: the Christian Church (Tradition); human reason; and the Bible. Then proceed with these questions that allow participants to supplement their workbook exercises:

Concerning "Tradition" and "Reason" as authorities:

1. What was the motive behind the tradition—additions to the law—formulated by the Pharisees?

2. Based on your study of Mark 7, why is excessive reliance on human tradition a problem in Christian living?

3. How did Jesus' response to the Sadducees' argument against the resurrection show the unreliability of human reason as a basis for authority?

Now shift participants' attention to "The Inspiration of Scripture" section. Ask:

1. How does I Peter 2:21, 22 help refute the so-called Kenosis Theory?

2. In view of the total biblical revelation we have about Jesus Christ, why is the Accommodation Theory illogical?

3. Why is it so helpful to survey what the Bible says about its own reliability?

RESPOND: Refer everyone to the "Practical Application" section. Write the following maxim on the overhead or chalkboard:

> MANY PEOPLE ARE BIBLICALLY EDUCATED
> BEYOND THEIR OBEDIENCE.

Ask: How does this statement relate to James 1:22-25?

Finally, pair off again, instructing each person to share with his or her partner the potential avenues of service he or she checked in the last workbook exercise for this lesson. After everyone describes the service opportunity God may be asking them to consider, have the other partner pray for its eventual implementation and fruitfulness.

Lesson 4

FOCUS: The late Vance Havner knew how important it is to

have a biblical awareness of human nature. In his delight-
ful book, *Pepper 'n' Salt*, (Baker) he observed:

"We are trying to get young people to volunteer and say
'Here I am,' before they have ever said, 'Woe is me!'"

To start your exploration of Lesson 4, read aloud the
Havner quote. Then ask: What is the relationship between
Havner's comment and your study on the nature of the
human being? Havner's insistence on a "woe is me"
attitude reveals the necessity of having a clear view of our
own bankruptcy and sinfulness as a prerequisite for serving God.

DISCOVER: To cover the section "The Image of God in
Humankind," ask group members to use their completed
workbook exercises to discuss these questions:

1. In what ways do human beings reflect God's image?

2. What are the implications of this truth for an individual's self-esteem? For the personal ministry of evangelism?

For "The Fall of Humankind," instruct group members
to read Genesis 3 and to review their responses to the
study questions in this section. Next, cover the various
workbook questions in sequence, allowing volunteers to
share their findings. Encourage feedback from a large
number of participants rather than allowing one or two
more vocal individuals to dominate.

DISCUSS: As you zero-in even further to life application,
point out to the group that another area in which a realistic
view of human nature helps the believer is in the battle
against temptation. In *Stand Tough* , author Terry Powell
explains the value of a lifelong sensitivity to our sin
potential. Share the following excepts with your group
members, stopping after each to allow time for interaction
and comments.

When an awareness of your sinful nature sinks into

your mind and heart, several things begin to happen:
•You realize that knowing what is right doesn't automatically mean you do what is right. The will is involved in right-wrong decisions.
•You cultivate a healthy mistrust of your impulses.
•You depend more on the Lord's strength. Spiritual pride has less chance of getting a foothold in your thoughts.
•You feel motivated to learn all you can about resisting temptation.
•Your appreciation of Jesus and what He did on the cross increases. He knows all about the darker side of your character, and He still loves you.

RESPOND: Ask for feedback to each of the three questions in the "Practical Applications" section of the workbook. Close with a time of conversational prayer. Ask the Lord to cultivate within the group members a lifelong awareness of both their significance and sinfulness.

Lesson 5

FOCUS: Begin by asking the group: What are some of the things non-Christians may say about Jesus? (Ask participants to recall conversations they've had with unbelievers, and comments they've come across in the media. Put abbreviated responses on the chalkboard or flip chart.) After several respond, emphasize that one of the most common thoughts cherished by unbelievers is this: "Jesus was a good man." Point out that we live in a pluralistic, secular culture. A variety of ideas and opinions about Christ flourish. Note that the content of Lesson 5 can better equip members to defend their faith in Christ as God incarnate.

DISCOVER: The section on Jesus' pre-existence included references concerning Jesus' fulfillment of Messianic verses in the Old Testament. Ask: How does it make you feel to know that Jesus' earthly life was a direct fulfillment of Old

Testament prophecies?

To cover the section on "His Humanity," ask:

1. What various evidences for Jesus' humanity did you uncover?

2. Why is it important to acknowledge His humanity, anyway? Have everyone turn directly to Hebrews 2:14-17 and 4:14-16 for reference.

Next, refer the group back to the question asked during the focusing activity. Draw their attention to each of the unbiblical notions which were listed and ask them to use discoveries made in the "His Deity" section of the workbook to show the inconsistent nature of each opinion. If an answer to the following question doesn't surface during this exercise, ask: In light of the Scriptures you examined, why is it illogical to insist that Jesus was just a "great moral teacher?"

DISCUSS: Remind learners of the four categories of evidences for Jesus' deity as outlined in the workbook. Then discuss:

1. Which evidence of Jesus' deity is most convincing to you? Why?

2. Which type of evidence would you use if you were engaged in either a formal or informal debate with a skeptic? Why?

RESPOND: Acknowledging Jesus' claim to deity should result in both allegiance and praise on our part. One way to keep this lesson from being too academic is to participate in corporate praise of the Lord. Here's a suggestion:

Perform a choral reading of Colossians 1:13-18, a passage highlighting the person and work of Christ. Repeat the reading twice, following this procedure:

    1. Verse 13—one male voice

2. Verse 14—everyone in unison
3. Verse 15—one female voice
4. Verse 16—everyone in unison
5. Verse 17—one male and one female voice together
6. Verse 18—everyone in unison

Go through the process of practicing the parts before the final reading. A "trial run" will enable the participants to communicate the text clearly and powerfully.

Lesson 6

Focus: Relate the following incident which occurred in a Christian school classroom:

A kindergarten teacher was determining how much religious training her new students had. While talking with one little boy, to whom the story of Jesus was obviously brand new, she began telling about His death on the cross. When asked what a cross was, she picked up two sticks and fashioned a crude one, explaining that Jesus was actually nailed to the cross died there. The little boy, with eyes downcast, quickly acknowledged, "Oh, that's too bad!" In the very next breath, however, she related that Jesus rose again and that He came back to life. As his little eyes got as big as saucers, he lit up and exclaimed, "Totally awesome!"
-Charles Swindoll, *Growing Deep in the Christian Life* (Multnomah Press)

Totally Awesome! That's the heartfelt response you want group members to have as a result of their survey of Jesus' life and ministry. Follow up the opening story by asking: Why does increased familiarity with the story of Jesus tend to stifle our sense of wonder and awe?

Before moving to the next phase of the lesson, pray together. Ask the Lord to give participants a fresh, child-like perspective on the content of this lesson.

Discover/Discuss: Because of the extensive amount of

material in the workbook survey of Jesus' life and ministry, it is unrealistic to go over every single Scripture reference and related assignment during this meeting. Neither is such a procedure necessary, since most of the observation exercises are self-explanatory.

However, it is important that everyone have an opportunity to raise questions about particular items of interest. Divide into groups of two or three persons. Give each group a copy of the following discussion questions. These questions provide an opportunity for participants to share meaningful insights they uncovered and will enable them to assist one another in deepening their own written responses. Circulate among the groups, sitting in, listening, and giving help when asked.

1. Which aspect of Jesus' life and ministry is most meaningful to you? Why?

2. Which workbook section offered the newest or freshest insights about Jesus? Explain.

3. What was the most encouraging truth you uncovered? Why?

4. What content area you surveyed has the most significant implications for our future ministries as believers? Explain.

5. Which assignment in this lesson caused you the most problems? Why?

Before moving to the final phase of the lesson plan, check with the entire group to see if anyone still has unresolved questions about any of the workbook assignments. Use material from your own study to clarify and resolve those areas.

RESPOND: The "Your Response" workbook section instructed learners to examine Psalm 103:1-14. This passage lists benefits of a relationship with God which now accrue to us on the basis of Jesus' accomplishment on the cross. Ask for volunteers to share the words/phrases from Psalm 103 which increase their appreciation for Christ. Close with a time of conversational prayer, allowing group members to publicly thank the Lord for one or more of the benefits He has provided.

Lesson 7

FOCUS: Read aloud the following comment, attributed to Henry Varley: "The world has yet to see what God can do with a man who is fully and wholly consecrated to the Holy Spirit." Then point out that Dwight L. Moody, the 19th century evangelist equivalent of Billy Graham, heard Varley's statement and vowed to be such a man. To provide transition to the lesson, emphasize that the same Holy Spirit who transformed D. L. Moody can change and use any individual who is willing.

DISCOVER: The workbook provides extensive coverage of the major biblical truths related to the Holy Spirit. Rather than rehash every single Bible passage and related assignment provided in the workbook, implement the following to develop creative expression:

Divide into groups of three or four persons. Give each group a magic marker, a couple sheets of poster board, and construction paper. Instruct members of each group to skim the Bible study content for this lesson, then work together to creatively capture one or more truths from the workbook. Tell each group to write a poem, create a bumper sticker, or make up a three minute skit that coveys the truths they would like to share about the Holy Spirit uncovered in the lesson. Give the groups twelve or fifteen minutes, then reconvene and have each group share their project for the benefit of everyone.

DISCUSS: Next, use the following list of questions as a more comprehensive way of reviewing and clarifying the lesson content. Ask several persons to volunteer responses to each question before moving to the next one. Feel free to insert your own insights, or add commentary to their contributions.

1. At this stage in your Christian experience, which truth about the Holy Spirit is most meaningful to you? Why?

2. Which was the freshest, "I-never-knew-that-before" truth you uncovered?

3. Which concept related to the Holy Spirit did you find most difficult to comprehend?

RESPOND: To conclude, remind everyone that the term Jesus used to describe the Holy Spirit was the noun form of the verb "to encourage." Translated "Helper" or "Comforter," the word Paracletos literally means "one who comes alongside." In small groups , have everyone share (a) one way God's Spirit has come alongside and ministered to him or her in recent weeks; and (b) one situation he or she will face in the near future in which the Holy Spirit's ministry will be needed in a special way. Members can then pray for one another in light of the needs shared.

Lesson 8

FOCUS: As a group, sing several hymns or choruses that focus on God's provision of salvation or Jesus' sacrifice on the cross. Have a member accompany on the piano or guitar.

DISCOVER: To review material in the "God's Provision of Salvation" section: Meet in groups of three or four persons. Instruct members of each small group to cooperatively write a "Thank-You" note to the Godhead which acknowledges the contribution each Person of the Trinity made in bringing us salvation. Each group will compose one note as a means of reviewing or restating the Bible study insights recorded in the workbook. Give each group about ten minutes before regathering. Then ask a representative to read aloud the group's "Thank-You" note.

To cover the "Our Response to God's Provision" workbook section, use the following series of questions to probe the participants' understanding of concepts presented:

1. What are some evidences—even among believers—that sin is taken too lightly?

2. What are some misconceptions that people often have about the concept of "repentance?"

3. How do workbook assignments in this section refute the idea that repentance is merely "feeling sorry"?

4. In his treatment of "trusting Christ personally," the author referred to Jesus' commentary in John 3:14, 15 about the event involving snakes, recorded in Numbers 21:4-9. What truth about salvation did Jesus point out from that event in Israel's history?

Discuss: In the discussion time, focus on the five reasons for assurance from I John. Ask different volunteers to describe the basis of assurance provided in each of the five references. Then prompt discussion by asking: Which basis of assurance is most meaningful to you personally? Why? Who can illustrate the presence of one of these "evidences of conversion" from your own experience, or from the life of a Christian you know? What do the evidences of salvation gleaned from I John say about the nature of true faith?

Respond: The "So What?" workbook section encouraged learners to think through ministry responses to lesson truths. At this time, ask for several volunteers to share the names of one unsaved person for whom they are particularly burdened. Ask other learners to pray for the personal relationships mentioned and for an opportunity to share the means of salvation with the unbeliever.

Lesson 9

FOCUS: Use the following excerpt from Warren Wiersbe to introduce this lesson. Then briefly elaborate on it from your own understanding, accentuating the importance of understanding the vocabulary associated with a Christian conversion experience.

Some Christians say, "Don't bother me with doctrine; just give me the beautiful devotional thoughts of the Bible." But if devotion is not based upon correct doctrine, it is shallow, and it is not going to accomplish anything. It is merely shallow sentiment . . . . When you understand [doctrinal] words, you are able to live what they teach. When we understand key words of the Christian life, then we know what a Christian is, what God has done for us, and what God wants to do for us.
-Warren Wiersbe, *Key Words of the Christian Life* (Victor Books), pp. 5, 6.

DISCOVER/DISCUSS: To cover the concept of justification, go through the Bible study exercises in this part of the workbook in sequence. Ask volunteers to contribute their written responses, and supplement their responses as you deem necessary. Next, use the following quote, again from Warren Wiersbe's book, to stimulate discussion and deepen your learners' grasp of justification:

Justification is an act, not a process. No one Christian is more justified than any other Christian. If you are saved and your sister is saved, your sister and you are justified in the same way, and you have the same righteousness . . . . We do not justify ourselves, it is God who justifies us (p. 15).

In order to deal with the material on the concept of adoption, ask for volunteers to again contribute their responses to the questions in this section of the workbook.

Encourage group members who have not yet taken part to contribute at this time. And once again, use an excerpt form Wiersbe's fine book to prompt discussion and increase their appreciation of this benefit of salvation:

What is adoption? . . . . Adoption is not the way you get into God's family; adoption is the way you enjoy God's family. Adoption is the act of God by which He gives each of His children an adult standing in His family. The instant you were saved, you received an adult standing, which means you have all the adult privileges. You also have adult responsibilities (p. 30).

To cover the concept of sanctification, first give a 5 minute lecture on its three aspects revealed in Scripture:

(1) Positional sanctification occurs whenever a person receives Christ. Because Jesus Christ was a perfect sacrifice for our sins, His righteousness was placed on our account. Positionally, God sees the believer as holy, clothed in the righteousness of Christ. This type of sanctification never changes.

(2) Practical, or progressive sanctification refers to the daily process of spiritual growth toward Christlikeness. We "progress" in sanctification, or holiness, to the extent that we choose to use the resources God has made available to us. So this type of sanctification is in part dependent on our daily decision and actions of obedience to His will and Word.

(3) Perfect sanctification will take place only when Christ returns. Only then will our thoughts and actions perfectly conform to the character of God.

Next, meet in groups of three to cover the relationship of faith and works. Instruct each triad to work together with crayons and construction paper to create a visual art sketch which shows the biblical relationship between "faith" and "works." This sketch should symbolically indicate the relationship between works and saving faith, as defined by the workbook author. It should include few words, except labels such as "salvation," "works," or "faith," which are acceptable. The aim is to creatively illustrate the concept rather than verbalize it. Then ask a representative from each group to display and explain its visual. (Use transparencies and an overhead projector for this exercise if possible.)

After each illustration is shown, encourage questions, comments, and discussion.

RESPOND: As a conclusion to this lesson, ask group members who have identified a prospective study partner to share his or her name. Pray publicly for those particular group members, especially for the conviction and discipline to follow-through on this ministry outlet after the course is completed.

Lesson 10

FOCUS: The following poem was written by a believer while in the throes of personal setback. He wrote it to a group of friends from his church who supported him emotionally and financially. Read it aloud to the group, then use the question that follows the poem as transition into this lesson.

INCARNATION

The load is heavy; my body is bent. My spirit, too, is weak and spent.

Darkness hovers, though the sun is high. Too tired to pray; too numb to cry.

Feeling hopeless—on a downward slide. Then you knock and come alongside.

Encouraging words, a listening ear, I'm reassured that Christ is near.

When pain turns the heart to stone, No one should have to go it alone.

In time and space, through thick and thin, God wraps His love in human skin.

Ask: What is the relationship between this poem and the subject matter of lesson 10?

DISCOVER: To cover "The Founding of the Church" workbook section, seek volunteer responses to the three written assignments (concluding with the question on Acts 2:42). As usual, encourage individuals to add to their own written responses pertinent information supplied by others.

To answer the following questions, instruct participants to draw from their workbook assignments in "The Nature of the Church" section:

1. In what sense is the nature of the Church "spiritual"? In what sense is it "universal"?

2. What are some practical implications of the universal aspect of Christ's Church? In what sense is the church a "local" identity?

3. According to Acts 14:23, what provision for local church life did God establish?

Workbook exercises in "The Ministry of the Church" section unveiled these four functions of the local church programming: teaching, fellowship, worship, and prayer. Rather than recap the biblical information members recorded in their workbooks, probe these four aspects of church life in relation to your local church. Here's a recommended procedure:

Put the four functions on the chalkboard or flipchart in a vertical column. Leave plenty of blank space for writing to the right and below each word.

Next, discuss the following questions, making notations on the board.

•Regarding TEACHING: What various instructional opportunities for adults does our church provide on a regular basis? (List all programs and activities that include

138

a teaching function.)

•Regarding FELLOWSHIP: What does our local church do to promote fellowship? What specific program activities or contexts do leaders provide which offer meaningful opportunities for cultivating fellowship? (List those.)

•Regarding WORSHIP: What are some elements of the worship services in most churches? What are some common hindrances to an individual's meaningful participation in a worship service? In what concrete ways can we better prepare ourselves for Sunday worship? (Again, list responses.)

•Regarding PRAYER: What applications do Ephesians 5:18 and II Corinthians 1:8-11 have for corporate prayer meetings in today's local churches? What program opportunities or meaningful contexts emphasizing prayer does our church put on the calendar?

Discuss: Upon completion of your discovery of the four church functions, encourage individuals to evaluate their participation in church life in light of the opportunities provided in your church program. Ask questions like: In what instructional opportunities of this church do I need to get involved, either as a teacher or learner? (And so on, with the other functions.)

For "The Mission of the Church" workbook section, divide into pairs. Have each pair review the Scripture references and assignments, then write a "Church Leadership Mission Statement" in 25 words or less. Let each pair read its statement aloud for the entire group, encouraging refinements.

Respond: In their workbooks, participants listed training events sponsored by your local church as well as opportunities offered by parachurch organizations and Christian colleges in the area. At this time, work together as a group to compile a "master list" of these opportunities in your area. Spend time reflecting on which opportunities seem most inviting.

Lesson 11

Focus: What misconceptions about angels, demons, or Satan have you read or heard? What accounts for these misconceptions? After volunteers respond, emphasize that erroneous views or a superficial understanding of spiritual beings abound because people in general neglect the only reliable source of truth: God's Word. We tend to rely more on human imagination about the supernatural than God's revelation on the subject. This lesson surveys biblical teaching which corrects the misconceptions people have about angels, demons, and Satan.

Discover/Discuss: To cover the subject of angels, the questions that follow aren't provided in the workbook. However, participants can glean information from their assignments in order to answer these questions:

1. What biblical evidence do we have of angels' existence? What information does Scripture provide about their nature? Their number? Their abode? Their future?

2. What various ministries did angels perform in biblical times?

Next, ask volunteers to describe times when they experienced the special protection or presence of God. They were instructed to think of such an experience in the "Ministering to Us!" section of the workbook.

For the section on demons, discuss:

1. What words best describe the nature of demons? 2. To which demonic activity does Paul refer in I Timothy 4:1?

3. What are some contemporary examples of "deceitful doctrines" which cause people to fall away from biblical teaching? (Examples might include Mormonism, New

Age philosophies, cults, even extreme forms of the "positive thinking" movement.)

To cover the subject of Satan, put the scrambled Bible verse that follows on the chalkboard: IS HEART HIS HUMILITY DOWNFALL A HONOR MAN'S BUT BEFORE PROUD COMES BEFORE Ask participants to unscramble it and write it correctly for their notes. Unscrambled: BEFORE HIS DOWNFALL A MAN'S HEART IS PROUD, BUT HUMILITY COMES BEFORE HONOR (Prov. 18:12).

Then discuss:

1. What is the relationship between the proverb and the information gleaned from Isaiah about Satan?

2. How does pride often surface in the life of a believer? In what sense are persons in ministry particularly vulnerable to the sin of pride?

RESPOND: Meet in groups of three or four persons. Have everyone to share with other group members their written replies to the last two questions in lesson 11 of the workbook. After each person shares his or her plans, encourage another member of the group to pray for his or her follow-through.

Lesson 12

FOCUS: Read aloud II Timothy 2:2. Ask: What leadership principle do we see illustrated in this verse? (The concept of "reproducing disciples." A leader's responsibility isn't merely to teach others, but to train them so they will become teachers as well.) What are some applications of this principle to this Truth that Transforms course?

DISCOVER: Give a mini-lecture (8-10 minutes) on the eschatological position held by your church and pastoral staff. Though the workbook author surveys the Premillen-

basis for it. (If you don't feel competent giving this mini-lecture, tape record an interview with your pastor on the subject and play it at this time.)

DISCUSS: Refer learners to the assignments in the following workbook sections: "The Return of Christ," "The Resurrection," "The Judgments," and "The Future in Present Tense." Most content uncovered in these sections is acknowledged by all evangelical Christians. Don't review every assignment in those sections, but do seek feedback to the following questions:

1. What questions that you've had about the end times did workbook assignments help resolve? Explain.

2. What questions on the subject of last things remain after completion of the workbook? (Try to resolve serious questions that arise. But point out that it is impossible to resolve all questions on this topic in just a few minutes. Refer persons who want to delve deeper into eschatology to pertinent books from your church or community library.)

RESPOND: Once again, refer group members to the principle of reproduction in II Timothy 2:2. Spend the rest of your session having group members think through the practical and realistic possibilities of discipling another person. How could they envision that happening in the future?